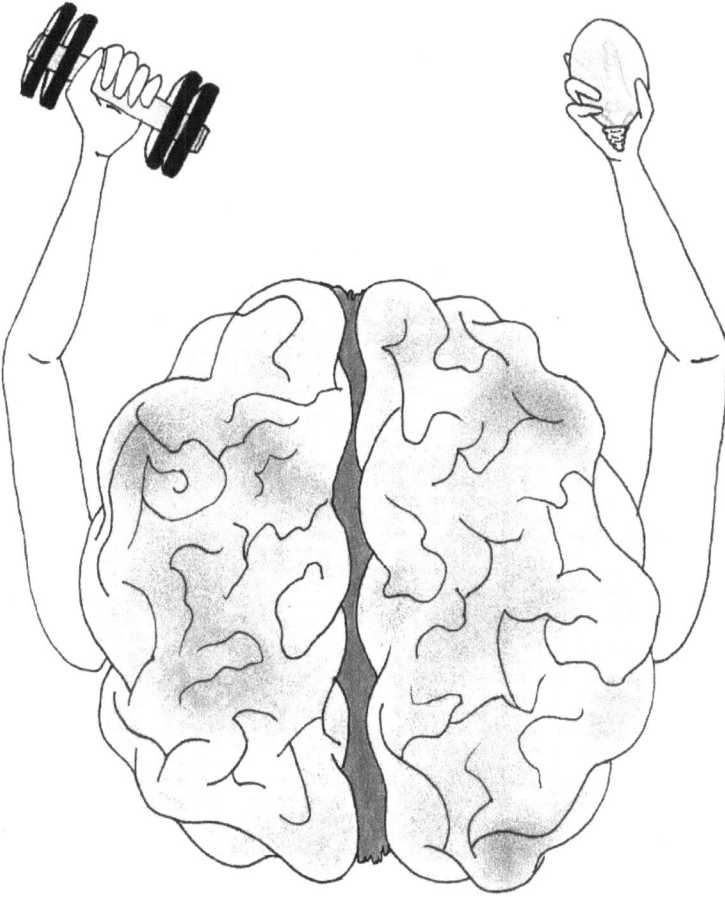

Learning

Understanding Oneself and Improving How We
Learn

Learning
Understanding Oneself and Improving How We Learn

Author: Shayne T Pattie

Cover Illustrator: Angela Pattie

Editors: Dr. Shellee Franssen and Peta-Jane Pattie

Indigenous Advisor & Contributor: Gayle Roe

Music & Learning Contributor: Claire Dickson

2024

Contents

Why this book and about the author

My name is Shayne and I currently live in north Queensland, Australia. I have always loved learning new topics from books and have been reading encyclopedias for fun from a young age. School was a great escape for me, and I was fortunate to have many supportive teachers. During adult hood, I found formal study at universities more challenging. Once I worked out how I learnt best, and what learning practices benefited me the most, I was able to begin completing study and learning objectives.

This book encompasses the many aspects of learning following my professional experiences in various fitness related fields including martial arts, personal training and Pilates. It has also been influenced by my experience as a psychologist helping other people improve their mental health and to learn new tools to improve other aspects of the overall health and functioning. I hope that this book will be a great reference book for people wanting to improve their ability to learn.

At present, I'm very engaged in my work as a psychologist, aiding people aged 8 and above in their journey towards improved mental and physical well-being. Alongside this,

I've delved into the realm of writing, crafting a book titled 'My Eclectic Human Body' which looks at the various facets of our physical selves and how we can enhance our health.

Within the pages of this book, I explore a range of ideas and perspectives on learning, offering readers different paths to better understand their own learning needs. As someone who sometimes struggles to recall where I learned certain information, I've made an effort to include references to the sources that have influenced my understanding. These references, found at the end of the book, service as signposts for those curious about the origins of the knowledge shared within.

Since this book is about learning, I have included some space for writing notes at the end of most subchapters. As some people retain information better if they have a chance to write their summaries as soon as possible. I have also chosen to use a slightly larger font size with increased line spacing, as learning research has suggested that a larger font size enhanced reading speed and accuracy of younger and dyslexic readers and I wanted this book to be as user friendly as possible.

What is learning?

Defining learning

Learning is defined by most dictionaries as "the acquisition of knowledge or skills through study, experience, or being taught". This starting definition helps to illuminate the idea of learning as being more than only remembering definitions. The word 'skills' is included, as a skill is something that can be taught theoretically, but also requires practice, leading to an improvement in that behaviour or task. The skills need to be tested and practiced allow the learning to be improved and embedded, leading to even deeper learning and more accurate memory.

Learning is also discussed as an increase, often through experience, of problem-solving ability. Researcher and author Washburne developed a formula they used to attempt to measure learning in a quantifiable way. Washburne's formula of m/r meant that 'm' represented the memories which aided in the extension of experience towards the goal, and the 'r' represented the resistance to the attainment of the goal (such as habits, conflicting goals, etc.). Their research suggested that when the ratio m/r increases, learning is proportional to cue reduction. As will be seen in the book, there are many theories of learning and goals, each with their own strengths.

Another important aspect of learning that is often overlooked is motivation, also known as 'the why'. This will be discussed later in the book, but it is important to raise this point here. When a person or team understands why they want to learn something or improve, they are more likely to work towards this. Alongside an individual's motivation is their perception. No one sees the world exactly as it is. Every person has their own perception based on their life experiences, their emotions and the context of the event or "thing" which influence how they understand and therefore how they respond to their reality.

Many of the learning theories discussed in this book will be rooted in a Western cultural viewpoint, informed by both my personal experiences and professional insights.

To assist in any form of learning, healthy eating, sleep and other positive life practices are beneficial, but will not be discussed in this book due to the focus being specifically on learning. However, this is an important side note, as we don't learn in isolation, and our ability to learn is directly influenced by our health.

When and how we learn

We learn every day, often known as informal or implicit learning. We learn when we speak to other people, we learn by reading, participating in activities, repeating the same task, attempting a new task, we even learn when watching a cartoon or movie. Our brain is always adapting and as a result we are always learning even if we are not aware of this fact. Even when asleep, we are still learning as our dreams act as thought and experience consolidation, as well as assisting in emotional processing and reorganising of the day's events.

This book will focus more on formal learning also known as *structured learning or learning with intent*.

When thinking of formal learning one of the first ideas people may remember is that of formal schooling. For many people daycare is their first example of formal learning, often taught to children through play or in primary school often taught in classrooms. This semi-structured and later structured learning environment is used to help teach many people the basics that their state or country has legislated as required learning. The modern-day school helps many people learn basic mathematics, language, science, and health concepts often through wrote learning and visual learning. The modern school is also a common place where young people learn social skills and emotional skills from their teachers as well as from other peers.

Understanding how we learn is useful as this knowledge can be used to improve our efficiency at learning. Another important aspect is our retention of our learnings.

Memory Summary

Memory can be defined as the mental capacity of retaining and reviving information including facts, events, emotional impressions, etc. Memory forms part of a person's perception of their reality but is not 100 percent accurate. When memories are being encoded, they can be impacted by various internal and external influences such as our own emotion, any relevant life history prior to the event or information, the context of the event or information, the event or information itself as well as various other sensory inputs. Memories can be encoded as various types, most of which have a strong overlap with each other including interpersonal (between people), intrapersonal (understanding of self) memory, fact or information-based memory, emotional memory, and somatic memory.

Somatic memory is when the person's body remembers the event or information physically such as a muscle tension response when the person sees an animal they fear, or a release of tension through a relaxing sigh when a person remembers a positive event from the past.

As well as somatic memory there are other types of memory known as Short-term memory, Long-term memory and Working memory. Short-term memory is a term used to describe the information a person can remember for a short period of time, often 15-30 seconds. Traditionally this often includes seven items of information plus or minus two, such as writing a short list or writing a person's phone number. Working memory often lasts up to 15 seconds and is the information the person is receiving. The level of focus and investment from the person during this time can greatly impact the accuracy and manipulation of information that is transferred to short or long-term memory. Long-term memory happens when the short-term memory is stored for longer term use and can include information that is older than 30 seconds. As will be seen throughout this book there are various ideas and frameworks in which academics and researchers have theorised we learn, store and retrieve memories.

There are various areas of the brain responsible for memory and the type of memory can influence what part of the brain is activated. The most common brain areas used in memory activation include the – Prefrontal Cortex, Neocortex, Basal Ganglia, Amygdala, Hippocampus and Cerebellum.

Different types of memories often require an activation from different brain areas. Explicit memories that can include direct experience and facts, often activate the Hippocampus, Neocortex and the Amygdala. Implicit memories such as motor memories often activate the Basal Ganglia and the Cerebellum. Working memory relies heavily on the Prefrontal Cortex and is therefore vulnerable when a person is under intense stress, or their environment provides a sensory information overload (which can also trigger a stress response).

The idea that the brain has memory types is a practice that we have developed to understand and compartmentalise our new and old understandings. The brain regions don't stick to their "type of memory" but instead there is often communication across the brain regions. Memory has been broken into the three types to assist in learning the basics only.

Notes:

Pre-learn, learn and drill

I chose to place this theory of learning towards the beginning of the book, as I felt it was a nice introduction into a learning idea that would benefit and be benefitted by some of other learning ideas in the book. Young and colleagues found that learning efficiency benefited from three core aspects he defined as Pre-learning, Learning and Drilling. His research found that Pre-learning was a helpful tool to assist a person in mapping or planning their learning journey. Pre-learning consists of identifying what the person wants to learn, planning what the most efficient and effective way to achieve the goal might be, the best order in which to learn (considering any prior learning that might need to be done) and identifying the most important things to learn with the relevant context. Other research has supported this and suggested that Pre-learning is a useful tool, but no more than 10 percent of the entire allocated learning time should be allocated to Pre-learning. This is theorised to avoid the possible procrastination that might occur during the Pre-learning phase.

Young identified the most important aspect of Learning that needs to be remembered was hard work. A person must spend the time and put in the effort to improve their learning. This can be made more efficient by removing external distractions (noise, other sporadic wants, etc.) and by removing internal distractions (what was for dinner, stress, anxiety, etc.). As discussed in other areas in this book, understanding the value and motivation behind the learning goal can assist in removing the distractions.

Finally Young discussed the term 'Drilling'. Drilling includes understanding what current weaknesses the person has that is relevant to the main goal but needs to be strengthened prior to the official learning taking place. It is thought that by strengthening the weaknesses, the rest of the learning journey and memory retention of the topic would be improved.

Using Young's structure can assist in improving how efficiently a person learns, even if it feels like it might take longer due to the Pre-learning process. Another important aspect is understanding how any other prior learning can assist in the learning process. Some researchers have used the term 'Lateral thinking' or 'Lateral learning' which can be loosely defined as the ability to use other information from topics that might not seem relevant to improve the outcome of the current goal or behaviour. One example in psychology might include using a physics example of 'Just Noticeable Difference' and instead applying it to goal setting and behaviour change.

Notes:

Learning Styles

There is some debate among academic circles regarding the efficacy of learning styles. The term 'Learning Styles' was made popular during the 1960s following the theory of Multiple Intelligences from Howard Gardner. Since then, there was a strong focus, almost to the extreme about learning specific ways. Some research has suggested that learning styles are irrelevant, and it is the person's determination and passion that determine if they will learn the desired goal. However, I strongly suggest that learning styles are relevant, but should be incorporated alongside passion and determination when learning. Understanding a person's motivation will assist in directing their passion and determination alongside their learning styles.

Many people don't learn with only one learning style, and often have multiple areas of strength when learning. For example, a person who studies for an exam by reading the content aloud while audio recording their own voice is implementing visual learning, auditory learning, and elements of kinetic and wrote learning. The learning styles a person uses, may also change based on the context of the learning, i.e., from a book in a library or in the middle of a busy workplace. There are many different learning styles that will be discussed with different academics using different terms for similar interpretations, which may lead to overlap across the learning styles.

Informational learning

Informational learning can include linguistic and mathematical subsets. The linguistic learning subset will often involve learning through words and can have a strong overlap with the verbal and auditory learning styles. A Linguistic learner utilises language as their foundation for most learning.

Mathematical learners often learn better with numbers, structure, and reasoning. The Mathematical learning style has a strong overlap with the Sequential and Aural learning styles. People who utilise the Mathematical learning style often have a strength in Informational Learning, and often work in engineering or similar fields. Some people who have this strength may also use this alongside their music learning or career.

Visual/Spatial learning

Visual learning refers to when a person learns by watching, reading, or seeing information or behaviours. The term

'Visual Learning' refers to the learner using their sense of sight to encode information or employ their internal ability to visualise the information. Today's technology allows visual learners to excel in many areas with an enormous amount of video content and electronic books available to the average person. Other examples include diagrams, flow charts, colour, and images.

This visual strength often translates to a better spatial awareness when performing physical tasks such as building.

Auditory learning

Auditory learning refers to when a person learns by hearing and listening to the discussed information and can include listening to the instructions of what is required for behaviours or outcomes. The term 'Auditory Learning' refers to the learner's ability to use their sense of hearing to process information by listening. This can include listening to a recording, debate, podcast, etc.

Verbal learning

Verbal learning involves using sound. Often this can involve a person reading text aloud, having group discussion, and interactive questioning of information. There is a strong overlap here with the Interactive and Aural learning styles.

Aural/Musical/ Rhythmic/Melodic learning

Aural or Music learning involves the use of rhythm and sound to assist in the learning process. The person may sing information or use musical melodies or rhythm while reading or speaking to assist in memory retention. A common example of this is the alphabet song, nursery rhymes and other learning songs. Aural learning also utilises subtle mathematic patterns or structure. Unfortunately, many westernised schools and workplaces often teach people that this style of learning is only for young children, leading to less effective learning when people move from primary school to high school and then to the workforce.

However, there has recently been improvements made in some schools, with some schools having entire music programs that utilise and encourage this learning strength as part of their core curriculum.

Kinaesthetic learning

Kinaesthetic learning refers to when a person learns by doing. This may involve physically attempting the behaviour or task or attempting to add a practical behaviour to a theoretical concept, such as building a solar system diorama when learning about space. It can also involve field trips, interactive experiments, and role-playing. Kinaesthetic learning helps activate the person's brain pathways and utilises the Proprioceptive and Vestibular senses which may be beneficial for some people.

Tactile learning

Tactile learning involves touch. This often involves the learner touching and manipulating objects to assist in learning. Examples of this can include the use of playdough to roll and make letters, shapes, numbers, etc. Science experiments in the classroom are a common Tactile learning tool. There is a strong overlap between Tactile and Kinaesthetic learning.

Sequential learning

Some people learn best when information is presented in specific orders. This can include alphabetical order, progress order, timelining and can also include flow charts. A common example is seen in public and school libraries where the Dewey Decimal system is used to display books, utilising a form of sequential learning.

Wrote learning

Wrote learning refers to the physical practice of writing information or completing a task enough times that the person can remember it effectively. This can still be seen today in formal education and is also used in sports, martial arts, and some trades. There is a strong overlap with Wrote learning, Tactile and Kinaesthetic learning, although some academics may disagree.

Reflective/Intrapersonal Learning

Reflective or Intrapersonal learning involves the person using their reasoning skills to solve problems and interpret complex information. This can involve brainstorming possible solutions to dilemmas, analysing material, and having discussions that explore deeper interpretations. Intrapersonal learners often find psychology, philosophy and other fields that require self-reflection easier and more interesting. The intrapersonal learner will also often be more aware of their own internal emotions and needs.

Interpersonal/Interactive learning

The Interpersonal or Interactive learning style often involves group type learning. Debates, group activities and any activity that involves another person can be beneficial.

This doesn't have to involve face-face learning and can also be done through question-answer scenarios or through open-source coding examples. This type of learning has a strong overlap with many of the other learning styles and is considered by some people, a practical example of combining different learning styles.

Implicit/Indirect learning

As discussed earlier, implicit learning often happens without our full conscious awareness, and is known as a "nonintentional automatic learning mechanism". Implicit learning may occur when a person fails an attempt, through social conversation, or from watching fictional movies. Implicit learning includes indirect (reading, etc.) and direct (life experience). Field trips, and apprentice programs can also be examples of this learning style. This implicit learning often happens slowly and can assist a person in developing what they may refer as "common sense". Some researchers also suggested that "muscle memory" is an example of implicit learning.

As a side note, the term "Implicit learning" can be helpful, however, terming it "common sense" may become unhelpful. Common sense as a term is often used in negative connotations but can be explained as 'assumed knowledge'. If a person can frame their previous implicit learning as 'assumed knowledge', it can allow them to appreciate their own life experiences without negatively impacting another person's.

Learning Styles Summary

As can be seen there are many different learning styles that with different academics using different terms for similar interpretations. Despite differences in terminology and opinion, advocates for the learning styles agree that a multisensory approach is best and where possible the learner, teacher, facilitator, etc., should implement a combination of learning styles. Understanding that the learning styles are useful frameworks rather than strict boxes can also be beneficial. Examples of multisensory learning includes group presentations utilising movement, PowerPoint, etc., drawing images and flow charts, and writing and performing songs, skits, etc.

Notes:

Sensory Impacts/Barriers for Learning

Sensory and Senses Introduction

There are various theories about how many senses we have. Some academics and researchers suggest that humans can experience up to 53 different senses, some say 33 senses, but most agree that people experience their reality through approximately eight main senses. The 53 senses theory was developed with work from Guy Murchie and Dr. Michael Cohen and separated our senses into multiple areas – Radiation Senses, Feeling Senses, Chemical Senses and Mental Senses. The 33 senses theory was developed with work from Diane Ackerman and Lorin Roche. Their work separated our senses into nine areas – Vision, Hearing, Smell, Taste, Touch, Pain, Mechanoreception, Temperature and Interoceptors.

Knowing as many senses as possible can be helpful for people wanting to achieve deeper meditation and deep understanding of self, however, for most people understanding the basic eight senses is enough. The main eight senses discussed in the rest of this section include – taste, touch, sight, sound, smell, proprioception, vestibular and interoception.

There are various 'Sensory Models', including Dr. Winnie Dunn's model, and Dr. Ayre's Sensory Integration model. However, due to my own professional training, I will be utilising the model from Dr. Miller's, 'Sensory Modulation Model'. This model separates a person's sensory difficulties into 'Sensory Sensitive', 'Sensory Slow' and 'Sensory Seeking'. A person can be 'Sensory Sensitive' to a type of stimuli but also use a variation as a seeking behaviour, however, it is most common that a person who is 'Sensory Slow' will also be 'Sensory Seeking' with that same sense.

Sensory Sensitive

'Sensory Sensitive' is defined as a sensitivity to a particular sense, often causing discomfort or distress. It can include – Only eating familiar foods, disliking strong tasting lollies, gag reflex when presented with new foods, disliking most fragrances from perfume or bath products, distress at smells that other children do not notice, disliking bright lights, greater than normal distress in unusual visual environments (e.g. bright colourful room, wall decorations), discomfort with fast moving images on television or movies, preferring the blinds/curtains closed, easily distracted visually, disliking loud, unexpected sounds (sirens, school bells), might cover ears or cry when presented with loud noises, larger than average startle response to unexpected sounds, easily distracted by background noises such as television or music, difficulty with higher pitched sounds such as hand driers, disliking having messy hands, disliking haircuts, disliking specific food textures, disliking specific fabrics, disliking teeth brushing more than other people, avoiding swings or trampolines, fear of heights and disliking feet off the ground and/or travel sickness or motion sickness. Ideas that can help with 'Sensory Sensitive' related difficulties include packing meals that are blander and serve sauces on side, using fragrance free washing detergent, having dark spaces for relaxing zones, using specific music or sound frequencies played through headphones, using vibration or heavier touch contact, using slow linear and rhythmic movements, and many more.

Sensory Slow

'Sensory Slow' is defined as being under responsive to sensory stimuli, often leading to seeking behaviours. It can include – Not noticing or care if food is spicy or bland, being unable to distinguish between different smells, not noticing noxious/ dangerous/ offensive smells, seeming oblivious to details of an object and the surrounding environment, not noticing when others walk into or leave a room, walking into objects or people as if they were not there, not responding when his or her name is called, not hearing sounds in the environment, appearing as if in their own world, making their own noises for fun (can also be related to stimming), not noticing if hands or face are messy or dirty, being unaware of temperature changes, not noticing if bumped or pushed, bumping into things or falling over objects, losing balance unexpectedly when walking on an uneven surface, having poor muscle tone or appearing more floppy than people of similar age, having poor endurance, becoming tired easily especially when standing or holding the body in one position, leaning on walls or slumping on furniture and/or walking loudly as if feet are heavy. Ideas that can help with 'Sensory Slow' related difficulties include cooking with sour or sweet flavours, using specific fragrances or fragranced washing detergents, using movement combined with visual cues or activities, having uneven or faster beats or visuals, buying different textured clothing, using higher intensity exercise or circuit training, encouraging team sports with lots of movement use environmental reminders for basic tasks such as eating enough or sleep routines.

Sensory Seeking

'Sensory Seeking' is defined as behaviours that involve the person wanting more of that specific sensory input and spending energy in meeting this sensory need. It can include – Adding salt & spice to their food, preferring spicy food, putting objects into their mouth prior to playing with them, enjoying music and television at extremely loud volumes, making noise in the background while doing other tasks, smelling people, animals and objects, touching people to the point of irritating them, seeking vibration, jumping/crashing/spinning/swinging/rolling, rocking in chair, jumping on bed or sofa excessively, loving fast movement input and/or grinding teeth. The ideas that can help with 'Sensory Seeking' related difficulties often have a very strong overlap with the ideas that help with the 'Sensory Slow' ideas.

Sensory Summary

All people have different levels of sensory input needs. Some people's brains filter close to the right amount of sensory information, and this leads to the person experiencing minimal sensory related stress. However, many people have at least one of their senses that either are sensitive leading to a sensory related stress (also known as sensory anxiety) or are sensory slow requiring seeking behaviours to help find the sensory homeostasis. Understanding our own sensory needs can assist in our own learning journey but also help with communicating with people we might be assisting in understanding their own sensory needs. When a person's sensory needs are met, they are much more likely to want to learn and be able to retain the learnt information.

Notes:

5E Model of Instruction

The 5E model was developed as an approach to science teaching and learning. It was developed by the Biological Sciences Curriculum Study in 1987 with the goal to improve the experience of learners and the effectiveness of teachers. The 5E model was strongly influenced by a previous model for learning by Atkin and colleagues known as the Atkin and Karplus Learning Cycle. The 5E Model of Instruction consists of five teaching phases – Engagement, Exploration, Explanation, Elaboration and Evaluation. Each phase serves a specific function and overall, they aim to help the teacher provide a more coherent instruction, as well as assisting the learner to engage in the learning to better understand and retain the scientific knowledge. Research conducted in schools from different socioeconomic backgrounds, over the last several decades have supported the efficacy of the 5E model. Other studies have suggested that the model assisted in developing a better conceptual understanding of scientific ideas and models, had positive effects on general achievement in science, improved the level of learner's wanting to pursue further scientific study after school and led to a more positive attitude towards science.

The first of the five areas in the 5E model is known as 'Engage'. 'Engage' involves the teacher introducing a problem or event in a familiar context that the learners cannot yet explain with their current knowledge, because their current knowledge does not yet fit in with the new challenge or experience. As a result of this a cognitive conflict arises for the learner. This conflict plays an important motivational role and provides an opportunity to activate and elicit the learners' prior knowledge. From the cognitive learning perspective, this stage of the 5E model, is important because it addresses several processes which have been proven to be critical for enhancing meaningful, durable, and transferable learning.

Research from various academic, psychology, neuroscience and learning experts has shown that encouraging learners to recall relevant knowledge from previous courses or their own life experiences can facilitate the integration of the new material. Strategies such as asking learners questions specifically designed to trigger recall or providing learners with a relevant context can help them use prior knowledge to aid the integration and retention of new information. The research has stated time and again that prior knowledge plays an essential role in the processing and retention of new information. Information that learners need to learn, depends on what they already know because learning is a constructive process, building foundations of prior knowledge in their long-term memory. This foundational knowledge and memory then must be activated via prompting to become useful during the learning episode. This means that it must be activated in the long-term memory and enter the working memory when needed so that the learner can hold and manipulate the information.

When this manipulation happens, the new learning is generated with some pieces of the new information being connected to semantically related pieces of knowledge that the learner had retrieved from long-term memory. Following this, when the learner wants to retrieve what has been learned, they will be able to reconstruct the memories using the related knowledge from different learning episodes. Research has suggested that human memory does not store redundant information, instead using information that is already consolidated in long-term memory to build on new memories that share those features. However, many learners were found to have difficulty accessing their prior knowledge and required explicit opportunities to do so, often in the form of guidance from the teacher. This guidance also helps to protect against inappropriate use of prior knowledge or context.

Learning involves an assimilation process but also requires an accommodation process, where the prior knowledge and conceptual structures of the learner need to be fundamentally restructured to allow an understanding of the intended knowledge. Activation of prior knowledge with assimilation leads to memory updating, also known as learning. It is thought to be essential to activate prior knowledge because only memories that become activated are prone to change according to the cognitive neuroscience research. Once the assimilation, accommodation and activation processes have been used, a reconsolidation needs to happen, often guided by the teacher. This reconsolidation of learning combined with the appreciation of the real-life implications of the knowledge assists in long-term memory retention and more accessible knowledge for the future.

This 'Engage' stage of learning is hugely important for the cognitive and emotional/motivational dimensions involved in the learning process. It also allows for group discussions and cooperative learning, which are also important for socio-cognitive learning, which has been suggested to be more beneficial for both the teachers and the learners.

The second of the five areas in the 5E model is known as 'Explore'. The 'Explore' stage is about the guided inquiry activity that provides opportunities for students to address alternative conceptions and build new explanations that make sense to them. The 'Explore' stage is where the learner investigates phenomena, share their observations, suggest explanations, and discuss their interpretations. During this stage the teacher will facilitate, guide and scaffold the learners' thinking, which is what most effective teachers do anyway. This stage focuses on the promotion of connections between the learners' prior knowledge and the new information. To help the learner with the exploration of information, a guided inquiry-based approach is used, to assist in fostering thinking and sensemaking during the learning task. This is because people are thought to learn and remember better when they think about what they are learning in in terms of meaning, when they are prompted to connect information in ways meaningful to them.

The 'Explore' stage provides the learner with opportunities to reformulate their explanations by inferring them from new experiences and observations. According to the classical model of conceptual change by Posner and colleagues, after recognising conceptions are inconsistent in a new given situation, the learner needs to find an adequate new conception that successfully explains it. The new explanation must be able to be grasped by the learner and the learner needs to understand how it is consistent with prior knowledge. This can be completed with small groups, where the role of the teacher is to once again make sure the learner can help others to solve problems by building on each other's knowledge, ask questions to clarify explanations and suggest avenues that assist in moving the group towards the goal. Learning in the group setting also allows for cooperation in problem solving activities as well as debate/argumentation which has been suggested to enhance the learner' cognitive development in areas of learning, thinking, and reasoning. The teacher's role also requires careful guidance and extensive scaffolding to facilitate learning and may also include learning through investigation to assist in sensemaking, developing evidence-based explanations, collaborating and communicating ideas. Lastly, this stage provides the learner with opportunities to explore specific information, thereby creating a "time for telling", setting up the next stage known as the 'Explain' stage.

The 'Explain' stage is where the new concepts that had been grasped during the 'Explore' stage are formalised. This allows the teacher to formally introduce the concepts and help the learner to organise their new knowledge in a way that facilitates encoding and later retrieval of the information. Lots of learning related research has suggested that when the learner is provided with an organisational structure to fit new knowledge, they learn more effectively, when compared to being left alone to deduce this conceptual structure for themselves. In this stage the formalised definitions and explanations of the intended models and concepts are cooperatively built by the learner with the close guidance of the teacher.

The fourth stage of the 5E leaning model is known as 'Elaborate'. Activities in this stage require the learner to apply the concepts and procedures they have learned to solve new problems in new contexts. The new concepts offer the opportunity to prove they resolve the previous anomalies whilst also leading to new insights and discoveries for the learner. Activities in this stage also provide opportunities for the learner to transfer their new knowledge to a wide diversity of contexts. This is often done via exposing the learner to multiple contexts to promote deeper understanding and assist in abstracting the relevant features of the concepts and develop a flexible representation of the knowledge. By providing multiple contexts of applicability for the same overall concepts, it assists in creating several retrieval routes to access the learned information, which in turn increases the probability of the learner being able to find a match between the cues given in the transfer task and the stored memory. Extended practice is essential if something new is to be learned, especially if the goal is for the new knowledge to be retained over time and transferred to new situations.

The final stage of this learning model is known as the 'Evaluate' stage. The knowledge and abilities acquired by the learner are assessed through an activity that challenges their understanding. This has often been more subtly completed throughout the other stages, often informally through feedback and discussions, and is another form of learning. During the 'Evaluate' stage, the learner is often provided with tests or other forms of formal evaluation to determine the learners' level of understanding and abilities, whilst also serving as a tool for the learner to self-evaluate. Testing also provides another opportunity for the learner to retrieve information from their memory which in turn changes the memory and may increase the probability of successful retrieval in the future, through active repetition. Whilst testing has many benefits to the learners' memory and knowledge retrieval, it can cause some learners' distress which may negatively impact their ability to access the learnt information and negatively affect future memory and knowledge retrieval.

The '5E Model of Instruction' was designed in the late 1980's and then later adapted with the goal of improving a person's ability to learn more effectively and efficiently. The research that is used throughout the model believes that when the pattern of neural connections that represent a memory in the brain is reactivated, the brain experiences a new round of consolidations which works to strengthen and adapt the original memory with the newly learnt information through an active reconsolidation process. The model can be used in one-on-one settings but was designed for group use such as in classrooms.

Notes:

Illusion of learning

Illusion of learning is when a person is physically attempting to learn information or a behaviour, but their mind is no longer paying conscious awareness. It also refers to a person who believes they understand a topic or task, but the person only recognises it. An example would be when a person studies for an exam for six hours without breaks and later only remembers the first or last hour of their study. A practical example might be a person who is fixing a car engine, finishes their task and finds a small piece left over. This suggests that at some point in their fixing, their mind stopped paying conscious attention and they relied on their muscle memory to finish the task. A personal example of the illusion of learning is when I was attempting to study a psychology topic. After two hours of study, I noticed I was now paying attention to the physics behind how bees fly. It is important for a person to understand the difference between learning and retaining information (learning and therefor knowing it) versus being with the information or task but not retaining it (illusion of learning).

Understanding the term 'illusion of learning' can be helpful and can be utilised to improve a person's study behaviours and memory retention. A person can use structured and semi-structured rests to help their learning retention and focus. A structured example may include setting an alarm for 2 hours and having a timed break such as 20 minutes. When the 20 minutes is finished, the person then returns to the study or task knowing they only must attempt to focus for 2 hours. A semi-structured approach would be when a person is studying or attempting a task, as soon as they notice their thoughts are on any other task or information such as food, they have a timed break such as 20 minutes, and when the break finishes, they return to their task or study.

This can improve a person's efficiency with learning, which is especially important when there are pressures such as due dates, fast-paced online workshops, etc.

Notes:

Current Psychology Learning Frameworks

There is a long history of psychology investigating how people learn including behavioural learning theories, cognitive learning theories, conditioning, and various others. This section will discuss the most common ideas that I have discussed with clients or have observed in various psychological settings including Journey vs Destination, Motivational Interviewing, Positive Thinking, Neuroplasticity, Conditioning, Observational/Social Learning, Stages of Change, FAIL, Proficiency and Becoming Great and the Time to Change.

Journey vs Destination

The Journey vs Destination argument is relevant to learning and the answer or outcome is individual and often context based. In some psychological frameworks such as Acceptance Therapy, they encourage people to identify what their destination is, but then try to redirect the person's attention back to their journey to assist in enjoying or appreciating their journey. It is important to acknowledge the destination as this allows the person to understand what their efforts are working towards. The destination can be 10 years away, or it can be within a month. The many concepts discussed in this book outline how and why the destination is important. Another more common word used in place of 'destination' is 'goal'.

One aspect often overlooked in modern societies around the world is the journey. Most people who are considered successful discuss that they learnt more from their failures along the way to their success and that their destination changed several times. Despite this, modern societies often place a strong societal and often peer-peer pressure on achieving, and less focus on appreciating and sometimes even enjoying the journey. Enjoying the journey is about being present in the now, mindful of the experiences and appreciating the positive and acknowledging the negative. When a person is solely destination focused, they might miss opportunities to adapt, might miss opportunities to enjoy, and might miss opportunities to improve. This last point can be summarised with the song lyrics "life is what happens when we are busy making plans".

Notes:

Motivational Interviewing

Motivational interviewing is a client-centred counselling style used by professionals to encourage and guide behaviour change. It was originally developed by clinical psychologists William R. Miller and Stephen Rollnick and has had various updates to the framework. Most health professionals use the core principles of Motivational Interviewing, even if they don't use the formal structure of it. Motivational Interviewing can also be used by people in management positions to help understand and guide their staff towards a common goal.

The core principles of Motivational Interviewing include Expressing Empathy, Developing Discrepancy, Rolling with Resistance and Supporting Self-Efficacy. Expressing Empathy often involves conveying that as the listener, you understand some of their emotional experience even if you may not fully understand their individual experience. Often this involves listening for key thoughts, feelings, and statements of facts, normalising the person's responses to a difficult situation, reflective paraphrasing and phrases with genuine emotion.

Developing Discrepancy can include discussions regarding their future goals, barriers to improving, and discussions about what happens if nothing changes. Rolling with Resistance can include reframing towards more goal directed or positive language without arguing with the person who is seeking assistance. Finally, the listener or professional should try to encourage as much Self-Efficacy as possible to enhance a person's belief in their ability to begin, maintain or complete a task or behaviour. The four processes of Engaging, Focusing, Evoking and Planning are the practical steps the professional might use to assist the person.

One suggested structure within Motivational Interviewing that is used to improve the outcome is known as OARS. OARS stands for – Open-ended questions, Affirmations, Reflective listening, and Summaries.

Other tools used in Motivational Interviewing that won't be explored here can include Agenda Mapping (also known in other frameworks as mind mapping), Brief Action Plan, Elicit-Provide-Elicit model, Patient Dilemma focus (focusing on the concern and barriers to change), Evoking (exploring the Pros and Cons), Readiness Rulers (such as a 1-10 Likert scale) and various other goal frameworks, discussed elsewhere in this book.

Notes:

Positive Thinking

The idea of thinking positively has been discussed for thousands of years through various spiritual practices, each with their own interpretation and causal explanations. There was a scientific movement investigating the idea of positive thinking as a tool to improve health in approximately the 1940s and 50s. More recently there have been a plethora of books and self-help guides using the idea of Positive thinking. Positive thinking can be loosely defined as looking at the brighter side of situations and is related to positive emotions and other constructs such as optimism, hope, joy, and wellbeing. Positive thinking is a mental attitude that admits into the mind; thoughts, words and images that are conducive to growth, expansion, and success. The idea is that if a person can change the words they use, they not only influence their perception, but can directly influence their overall health including physical and mental health.

As mentioned in the book 'My Eclectic Human Body', a field of science known as 'Psychoneuroimmunology' has been investigating the idea of positive thinking through a scientific and slightly spiritual lens. They believe that the interaction of our conscious thoughts and emotions can directly influence our neurology, mental health, and immune system. An emotionally induced illness is physical (felt in the body) and not imaginary due to the mind-body connection. Research was demonstrated in 1975 and is now known as Biochemical Perception. Biochemical perception highlights what a person can do to change the negative biochemical responses to stress. How a person perceives an event, directly impacts our immune system, thereby affecting our emotional and physical health. This provides an understanding of the importance of managing internal and external emotional conflict. The biochemical perception is also about how our internal environment is affected by stress, and that our perception of this can influence whether the stress increases or decreases. Emotions have a direct impact on our immune system as the body communicates with the brain via bidirectional communication. This suggests that changing our language use from negative to positive or to goal directed language can improve our stress management.

Psychoneuroimmunology research has found that almost every cell within the body responds to the way we think. The emotional aspects of a person influence their physical manifestation as evidenced by how stress modulates the activities of the nervous, endocrine, and immune systems.

The physiology of hopefulness can help the body to fight disease, whereas longer term emotional stress quietly harms the immune system and other systems in the body. Nerve proteins known as neuropeptides affect our emotions as well as our physiology. A feeling in the mind will translate as a peptide being released somewhere in the body, as peptides regulate every aspect of the body including digestion and immune system responses. Neuropeptides' neuronal signalling of molecules influence the activity of the brain in specific ways.

Different neuropeptides are involved in a wide range of brain functions, including analgesia, reward, food intake, metabolism, reproduction, social behaviours, learning and memory. When we change the way we think, we can change the way we feel and this creates a perceptual change, which in turn allows for a deeper level of self-governance around our thinking. Every emotion has connection with a physical counterpart, and every ailment has an emotional attachment.

A researcher and author Candance Pert discussed that the body and mind are one and that what a person thinks and how they speak, directly impacts the state of the body's cells. The spleen, every lymph node, and all floating immune cells are in close communication with the brain. Emotions live and run every system of the body, and are in bidirectional communication with the nervous, endocrine, and immune systems. Our emotional state is directly affected by perception, suggesting that a negative mind will lead to an unhealthier body.

Our perception changes, life changes, etc. trigger an epigenetic response, meaning they change our genetic memory and gene expression. Genetic memory can be altered through the process of positive thinking and visualization (for those without Aphantasia), which stimulates a positive emotional state and adjusts to a negative one. Generating pleasant feelings helps a person to gain a sense of control, build hope, and increase the ability to generate and experience love, laughter, empathy, joy, confidence etc. The body's goal is homeostasis; however, the responses are not always accurate, and a stress response may be activated when there is nothing to fear, dependent on the emotions and thoughts a person is experiencing in the moments prior, during and following. Whilst the goal is to generate positive emotions and thoughts, to assist the body's health and recovery, we also don't want to suppress the negative emotions and emotional awareness. If we ignore our needs and suppress our emotions, our subconscious mind will alert us to the fact that something is wrong, which may result in a physical manifestation of emotional strain and medical illnesses. This highlights the ever-increasing importance of self-interventions.

As discussed, thinking positively can directly improve our overall health and mental health. Thinking positively is not about dismissing the negative impacts of an event, emotion, or thing, rather about helping a person gain some control over their health and responses. Changing our language towards positive or goal-directed does not mean ignoring or dismissing negative experiences. Rather, it means encouraging a person to acknowledge and learn from their negative experiences, and then find ways to change their language use, in order to improve their health.

Notes:

Neuroplasticity

Neuroplasticity involves the brain's ability to change by internal and external stimulus. It can be defined as brain's ability to change, remodel, and reorganise for purpose of better ability to adapt to new situations. Prior to 1890 it was commonly thought in many westernised cultures that the brain stopped developing after the first few years of life. It was commonly thought that only during the early "critical period" as a young child, that connections formed between the brains nerve cells which then remained fixed in place as we age.

As such it was considered that only young brains were able to change and thus able to form new connections. Because of this belief, scientists also thought that if a particular area of the adult brain was damaged, the nerve cells could not form new connections or regenerate, and the functions controlled by that area of the brain would be permanently lost.

However, in 1890 a psychologist William James, released his work known as the 'Principle of Psychology'. His work suggested that human brain including the adult brain was able to adapt and change, however his work was not widely accepted until 1948 when a neuroscientist Jerzy Konorski coined the term 'Neuroplasticity' and suggested that over time neurons that had 'coincidental activation due to the vicinity to the firing neuron would after time create plastic changes in the brain', meaning the brain can and will change. Again, it took time for this idea to be accepted by the scientific and psychological societies, taking until the late twentieth century. There is now a lot of resources discussing this importance.

Today, almost any educator, health worker, and most parents understand to various degrees, that the brain is capable of change. The brain is wired for survival and efficiency. The brain doesn't "care" about our long-term health, it "cares" about keeping us alive and being as efficient as possible. This is very useful as it allows people to learn about potential dangers increasing survivability and learn more efficient ways of performing tasks.

However, there are some negatives to neuroplasticity, with the first one being we are unable to directly choose how the brain adapts. As discussed in other sections of this book, we can influence our thoughts and our behaviours which has the side effect of changing our brain, but we do not have direct control. What we do, feel, and experience during the day is often consolidated and reorganised while we sleep.

We are all capable of change, so instead of letting the brain decide, it is useful to instead make positive life choices where we can, so that when the brain does its job of being efficient, we at least are having some positive input. This is also helpful to know for some people as it can provide hope that change is possible.

Notes:

Conditioning

One area of psychology that focuses heavily on learning is known as 'Conditioning'. There are two major types – Classical Conditioning and Operant Conditioning. Classical Conditioning often involves an involuntary response and stimulus where Operant Conditioning involves a voluntary behaviour and consequence. Operant Conditioning is focused primarily on behaviours under our conscious control and leaves the automatic and reflexive behaviours to the Classical Conditioning framework.

Classical Conditioning

Classical Conditioning is also known as Pavlovian or Respondent Conditioning because of the experiment first published by Russian physiologist Ivan Pavlov in 1897. Classical conditioning is a type of automatic learning that is created through associations between an unconditioned stimulus and a neutral stimulus. The most famous example involves Pavlov's dog food experiment. Pavlov conditioned his dogs through a process of associating sound (neutral stimulus) and food (uncontrolled stimulus). The original sound of the tone did not produce any greater amount of salivation from his dogs. However, after enough pairings of the sound with the food, when the dogs heard the sound, their brains associated the sound with food and created a greater amount of salivation in anticipation of the food.

In psychology a field known as 'Behaviourism' developed from this idea of classical conditioning and psychologists such as Watson and Rayner strongly led the way using research and experiments. There is some overlap between behaviourism and social learning, the latter of which will be discussed elsewhere.

The underlying principles in Classical Conditioning include – Neutral Stimulus (a stimulus that initially does not trigger a response until it is paired with the unconditioned stimulus), Unconditioned Stimulus (the feature of the environment that causes a natural and automatic unconditioned response such as dog food with Pavlov's dogs), Unconditioned Response (an unlearned response that occurs automatically when the unconditioned stimulus is presented), Conditioned Stimulus (a substitute stimulus that triggers the same response in an individual as an unconditioned stimulus), Conditioned Response (learned response to the previously neutral stimulus), Acquisition (an individual learns to connect a neutral stimulus and an unconditioned stimulus), Extinction (the gradual weakening of a conditioned response by breaking the association between the conditioned and the unconditioned stimuli/unlearning, such as the bell ringing without food being presented), Spontaneous Recovery (return of a conditioned response in a weaker form after a period of time post-extinction), Generalisation (tendency to respond in the same way to stimuli that are similar but not identical to the conditioned stimuli) and Discrimination (process through which individuals learn to differentiate among similar stimuli and respond appropriately to each one).

Classical Conditioning involves three stages – Before, During and After conditioning. The first stage involves the unconditioned stimulus eliciting an unconditioned response. This means that the stimulus in the environment has produced a behavioural response which is unlearned and therefore natural. The neutral stimulus in classical conditioning does not produce a response until it is paired with the unconditioned stimuli.

The second stage involves the originally neutral stimulus being associated with the originally unconditioned stimulus leading to relationship whereby the stimulus is known as a

'Conditioned Stimulus'. The third stage involves the conditioned stimulus now being associated with the unconditioned stimulus to create a new conditioned response.

Classical conditioning can often be evident in stress or trauma responses and in psychology is sometimes known as paired association. An example could include a person who eats chocolate often with no conditioned response, becoming ill, and then having a conditioned response such as nausea whenever they think of eating chocolate again. A trauma response might include a person is hit by a red car, and then has a fear response only to other red cars. Classical conditioning is also relevant, in part, with addiction, fear responses, taste aversions, organisational behaviour and classroom learning where a person learns a response that they previously did not have in relation to a stimulus that was previously neutral.

There were several flaws in Classical Conditioning, however, it formed a strong base in which many other areas of psychology were able to develop and further our understanding of the brain, mental health and learning.

Operant Conditioning

Operant Conditioning involves an association being made between a behaviour and a consequence (positive or negative). Operant Conditioning was first described by Skinner who was an avid and early proponent of behaviourism psychology. Skinner strongly believed that internal thoughts and motivations were not required knowledge and that we only needed to understand the external, observable causes of human behaviour. Skinner used the term 'Operant' and defined it as "an active behaviour that operates upon the environment to generate consequences", which was heavily influenced by the work of Edward Thorndike's 'Law of Effect'. Outside of experimental laboratory conditions, Operant Conditioning often occurs where reinforcement and punishment take place, such as classrooms, therapy sessions or team sports.

In a classroom setting, if a student who raises their hand is rewarded with helpful information or praise regarding their behaviour, they are more likely to raise their hand in the future. This is because their initial behaviour of raising their hand was followed by a reinforcement or desirable outcome leading to the original behaviour being strengthened. The opposite occurs when the original behaviour is followed by an undesirable outcome such as punishment or lack of response. Such as if a student tells the same joke and receives no laughter from their peers. This leads to the original behaviour being weakened/less likely to occur again in the future.

The key concepts in Operant Conditioning include Reinforcement and Punishment, with a third, less spoken about concept known as Neutral Operants. Reinforcement includes positive and negative reinforcers. Positive reinforcers are favourable events or outcomes that occur following the behaviour. A response or behaviour is strengthened by the addition of praise or a direct reward. Negative reinforcers involve the removal of an unfavourable event or outcome after the original behaviour. A response is strengthened by the removal of something considered unpleasant. An example of where both can happen involves a screaming child in a public setting. A child screams as they want a biscuit, when the parent gives them the biscuit under the condition of the child being quiet, the child's screaming behaviour is strengthened (screaming equals biscuit) and the parent's behaviour of providing the treat is also strengthened as the parent is rewarded with silence. When using Positive Reinforcement there is a concept known as the Premack Principle which states that any positive reinforcement should make use of a preferred activity (high-probability behaviour) as the reward for completing a less preferred behaviour (low-probability).

Operant Conditioning has two types of punishment – Positive Punishment and Negative Punishment. Punishment is a tool used to weaken or eliminate a response. Positive Punishment is the addition of an unfavourable event or outcome such as spanking. Negative punishment is a punishment through the removal of a favourable event or outcome such as a removal of a toy or opportunity. Ineffective Punishment may occur when the punishment being used is no longer decreasing the undesired behaviour. One example might include a parent that says no desert if the vegetables are not eaten, but the child forgoes the desert and still does not eat the vegetables. Whilst punishment is often easier to implement than reinforcement there have been several weaknesses found regarding its use including – the behaviour may not be forgotten only suppressed until the punishment is no longer present or effective, there might be an increase in aggression in an attempt to negate the use of the punishment, it might create fear regarding the undesirable behaviour but also anything connected to the behaviour, and it might not guide towards the desired behaviour as it may only teach what not to do instead of the desirable behaviour is.

Neutral Operants are often not discussed when exploring Operant Conditioning but are important to understand as they are variables that may subtly improve or hinder focus. Neutral Operants are the responses from the environment that do not increase or decrease the probability of a behaviour being repeated.

In Operant Conditioning the application of reinforcement has several different types known as different Reinforcement Schedules. The five schedules are known as Continuous Reinforcement, Fixed-Ratio Schedules, Fixed-Interval Schedules, Variable-Ratio Schedules and Variable-Interval Schedules. Continuous Reinforcement is defined as delivering a reinforcement every time a response occurs. This allows for the learning to occur quickly, however, also allows for the extinction (loss of conditioning relationship) to occur quickly once reinforcement stops. Fixed-Ratio

Scheduling involves a type of partial reinforcement. Responses are reinforced only after several responses have occurred. Fixed-Interval Schedules involves a partial reinforcement, but the reinforcement occurs only after a certain time interval has elapsed. Responses here remain steady and begin to increase as the reinforcement time draws nearer but may slow immediately after the reinforcement has been delivered. Variable-Ratio Schedules involves a type of partial reinforcement that strengthens a behaviour after a varied number of responses, which can lead to a high response rate and a slower extinction rate. Variable-Interval Schedules involve delivering reinforcements after variable times elapse, which can lead to a fast response rate and a slower extinction rate.

Two examples of Operant Conditioning leading to behaviour modification include Token Economy and Behaviour Shaping. A Token Economy is a reward system where desirable behaviours are reinforced with tokens (that form a secondary reinforcer) and are later exchanged for rewards (a primary reinforcer). This is often used in a classroom setting where teachers reward students who have demonstrated the desirable behaviour, with tokens or a tally that the student can exchange at the end of a term or semester. Behaviour Shaping involves the existing response gradually changing across successive trials towards the desired target behaviour through rewarding exact segments of behaviour. This requires the conditions to receive the reward to gradually shift closer towards the desired behaviour, and Skinner believed that human behaviour such as language learning was an example of Behaviour Shaping.

Conditioning Summary

Classical Conditioning formed an integral base for most of the subsequent behaviourism ideas and led to improvements in various areas such as animal training and factory work efficiency. However, when working with groups and individuals, Operant Conditioning has been found to be more effective at eliciting behaviour change compared to Classical Conditioning and when paired with more modern ideas that include motivation and values it can be used in almost all areas of human behaviour change.

Operant Conditioning had several weaknesses of its own including the dismissal of internal processes and the lack of social learning investigation. However, it still contributed a strong base of ideas that are still used in many modern learning programs.

Notes:

Observational/Social Learning

Observational Learning, also known as Social Learning, occurs through observing and imitating others. The most famous Social Learning theory came from Albert Bandura, who suggested that people learn through conditioning, but they also learn through observing and imitating the actions of people in their environment. One way of framing Observational Learning is "learning from others' experiences". If a younger sibling observes their older sibling receive a speeding ticket, the theory suggests the younger sibling would be less likely to speed when they drive.

Bandura's most famous experiment is known as the 'Bobo Doll' experiments. This involved people imitating the actions of other people without any direct reinforcement. Young people observed aggressive behaviours towards the inflatable doll and then imitated the aggressive actions of the adult. The children were not directed to act aggressively but were left alone with the doll after watching the behaviour. Bandura's experiments also then added an aspect of Operant Conditioning as they found that young people were more likely to copy the aggressive behaviours when the adult received no punishment or when the adult received a reward, versus being less likely to act aggressively when they saw the adult receive a punishment.

Observational Learning plays an important role in the socialisation process as it indirectly and directly teaches the young person which behaviours are recommended or not recommended. As humans are a social species, the socialisation process is one of the most important learnings that people learn to live a healthier life when they are adults.

There are four stages of Observational Learning – Attention, Retention, Reproduction and Motivation. For a person to learn something from an observation they must be paying enough cognitive attention and remain focused long enough for the learning from the model to be absorbed. Once absorbed, the learning from the model must then be understood enough otherwise the next stage of Retention is unable to happen. Retention happens when the person can recall what was observed, and if they can attach the reasoning behind the behaviour, their retention can be improved. Reproduction occurs when the person can replicate the observed learnings of the original model in a relevant context, even if the reproduction is not exactly the same as the original behaviour or learning. Finally, Motivation is important because even if the person meets the first three stages, if they are not motivated to continue the learnt behaviour or if they are motivated to discontinue the behaviour (such as observing punishment), the learnt behaviour will lessen or cease.

Neurologically speaking, Observational Learning makes use of a basic brain function known as mirror neurons. Mirror neurons are neurons which fire not only when an individual exhibits a behaviour, but also when observing a behaviour. Mirror neurons play a functional role in theory of mind, emotional recognition, empathy, acquisition of language, predicting intention, and imitation. Research has supported the idea that when a person looks into the eyes of another person and discuss difficult topics, over a short period of time, both people's brain waves become very similar, activated by mirror neurons which, in this context can impact a person's emotions and empathy. It has also been suggested that the emotion mirror neurons are stronger than motor mirror neurons. When a person's motor mirror neurons are activated our skin cells and pathways help us understand it is not happening to us. Emotion mirror neurons don't have a skin barrier or defence, meaning greater emotional brain-brain influence, often called empathy.

Whilst the Observational Learning model has been useful for many individuals and professionals regarding improving learning outcomes, there have been some areas of concern regarding its long-term impacts and real-world replication and validation. For example, some studies found that children who played violent video games were more violent. However, more recent studies have found that the children were not necessarily violent because of the video game but did have poorer emotional regulation and greater stimulation seeking which could increase the risk of aggression. Another real-life complication of Observational Learning is the "cyclic argument". Simply put the "cyclic argument" suggests that if a person observed their core parental figure to be an alcoholic, they would learn that this is the normal behaviour. On the surface this sounds accurate, however, it is specious thinking. The observed alcoholic behaviours become a risk factor for becoming a learnt behaviour and therefore becoming an alcoholic but do not then lead to alcoholic behaviours on their own. This is an important distinction often forgotten by many academics and Hollywood movies.

Observational/Social Learning is very useful, but like most learning frameworks discussed in this book, benefits from a combination of other information and learning ideas.

Notes:

Stages of Change

The Stages of Change was first developed to assist people with addictions to understand and improve their behaviours. The Stages of Change is also known as the Transtheoretical Model and developed by Prochaska and DiClemente in the late 1970s. Today we use the Stages of Change regarding most behaviour change related difficulties including addiction, fitness, health, finance, etc. The model is very useful for people to understand and explore their motivation to change and understand that change can be a lifelong challenge or practice. Often this model is used in professional settings such as psychological counselling, coaching, and in support groups.

The Stages of Change have six stages - Precontemplation, Contemplation, Preparation (Determination), Action, Maintenance and Lapse/Relapse. Precontemplation is that stage when a person does not understand or is not aware that their behaviour is negatively impacting their function. Often people in this stage can feel they and their behaviours are fine, and that if any issues arise, the issues are then externalised onto other people or environmental factors. Often support people can only provide emotional or other support and information but cannot provide direct guidance during this stage of change.

The Contemplation stage is when a person understands there might be an issue with their current behaviour. Often pros and cons regarding their behaviour begin, but change is not yet made as they may not yet have the motivation or still be ambivalent regarding making the change required. For many people going from this stage to the Preparation stage can be the most difficult due to the responsibility of previous behaviours that might be acknowledged.

The Preparation stage involves preparing to change. Often people are ready to make change within the next 30 days, and the person might begin to make small steps towards changing their behaviour. Often motivation and determination can be at its peak.

The Action stage involves people who have recently begun changing their behaviours and intend to keep moving in the forward direction with these changes. This can often look like a person modifying their previous unhealthy behaviours and/or beginning new healthier behaviours.

The Maintenance stage is when the person has sustained their behaviour change for a while, often more than six months, and they intend to maintain the new behaviour(s). For many people the Maintenance stage can become the hardest stage due to its long-term nature. This is even truer for many people with neurodivergence or trauma, as the Maintenance stage can represent a lack of stimulation and boredom. This can then lead to a lapse or a relapse into the previous unhealthy behaviour.

The final stage that can occur at any point between the first five stages is known as Lapse/Relapse. Often these terms are used interchangeably, however, understanding the differences can assist with future recovery and improvement. A Lapse can loosely be understood as when a person drops back a stage or two. The person might have made it to the Maintenance stage then a life stressor occurs, which might then lead to the person returning to the Preparation stage. A Lapse is common and natural and should not be seen as a failure, rather it should be seen as a response to a negative situation, and hopefully lead to better responses in the future. A Relapse is when a person might restart the entire cycle again. Often this occurs as a large response to a large stressor or life event. For example, a person who has not used alcohol for two years and is maintaining healthy behaviours might lose a loved one or a job or a limb. This massive loss can lead to previous unhealthy short-term behaviours such as alcohol use. This person is capable of change and can go through the stages again, and if they are fortunate, they might be able to go through the stages more efficiently with the life lessons learnt from their previous experiences. Often this person might require extra supports from professionals and support people to get from the Precontemplation to the Contemplation and Preparation stages.

There have been ten processes of change that have been found to occur and assist when a person is going through the Stages of Change. Different processes can have greater or lesser effect on a person's change depending on where they are on their journey. The ten processes are Consciousness Raising, Dramatic Relief, Self-Re-evaluation, Environmental Re-evaluation, Social Liberation, Self-Liberation, Helping Relationships, Counter-Conditioning, Reinforcement Management and Stimulus Control.

Consciousness Raising involves increasing the awareness about the healthy behavioural alternatives, Dramatic Relief involves the emotional arousal about the healthy behavioural alternative (can be positive or negative), Self-Re-evaluation is the self-reappraisal to realise the healthy behaviour is part of who they want to be, Environmental Re-evaluation is the social reappraisal to realise how their unhealthy behaviour affects other people, Social Liberation is the environmental opportunities that exist to show society is supportive of the healthy behaviour, Self-Liberation is the commitment to change a behaviour, based on the belief that achievement of the healthy behaviour is possible, Helping Relationships involves finding supportive relationships that encourage the desired change (these can be professionals, family, friends or support groups), Counter-Conditioning involves substituting healthy behaviours and thoughts for unhealthy behaviours and thoughts (and can lead to a lapse or relapse), Reinforcement Management is when the positive behaviours are rewarded whilst the negative behaviours receive less and less reward, and finally, Stimulus Control is the re-engineering of the environment to have reminders and cues that support and encourage the healthy behaviour and remove those that encourage the unhealthy behaviour.

There are several limitations to the model including – it can be ignorant of the social context in which changes occur such as Socioeconomic status; the lines between the stages can be vague with no concrete criteria to determine the person's stage of change; there is no concrete information about how much time is needed to reach and remain in a stage; and the model assumes that the person will make coherent and logical plans in their decision making process, which is often not the case as people are inherently emotional beings, more so when they are struggling. The Stages of Change model can be used as a very structured framework of behaviour change but can also be used more loosely as framework of ideas. Despite the limitations, the Stages of Change model has been found to be very helpful in changing unhealthy behaviours into healthier alternatives.

In the formal learning environment, the Stages of Change model can assist students and educators to identify if there are any less helpful behaviours or routines the person uses regarding learning. Once this is identified then the person (often with assistance from other people) is able to problem solve and work towards a new healthier alternative behaviour that will improve their learning efficiency and reduce their risk of a lapse or relapse.

Notes:

FAIL

Most people don't like failing and can be impacted by the possibility of failing. For some people it is helpful to see the word 'fail' as an acronym to help change the person relationship with the idea. The acronym FAIL stands for First Attempt In Learning. Some of the greatest human achievements were achieved after many failures such as the light bulb, flight and even children's entertainment such as 'Captain Underpants'.

Continuous failure with learning often leads to a person achieving something better than they originally set out to achieve. Failure is an important teacher for those who are willing to learn. When a person can change their internal dialogue and therefore relationship with the idea of failing, a failure changes from a long-term negative to an opportunity to improve.

If a person has sufficient support from their environment, it can greatly improve how quickly the person is able to recover and can also influence what information the person learns from the failure experience.

Notes:

Proficiency and Becoming Great

Proficiency

What is the difference between being proficient and being great? Proficiency is the ability to perform a task or understand and communicate information in a way that is accurate and efficient. Many people reach a level of skill where they become proficient and for some people this is enough. It is okay to be proficient in more than one area and never be great at it. The pursuit of becoming great is an individual want but is also encouraged by many cultures and subcultures around the world.

10 000 Greatness Hours?

There are many assumptions about what it takes a person to become great at something. Apart from the myriad of difficulties trying to define this, there are also individual differences that are discussed throughout this book. One idea of what it takes to achieve 'Greatness' is "thousands of hours of intensely focused practice and work, with the guidance of experienced people". That is probably the most well-rounded definition, however, one idea that is often used as an unofficial rule is the "10 000 hours" rule. This number was first used by Malcom Gladwell in his book

'Outliers: The Story of Success' in 2008. It has been used as a motivational number and a marketable number and can be considered an average at best. The general idea is that if a person practices for approximately 10 000 hours they will be proficient enough at the skill that they could be considered great.

Quantity of practice is important as it helps the brain pattern the required knowledge and skills so that they may become useable without too much conscious effort. Often known as "blueprinting" or "mechanical repetition", quantity of practice has been a helpful tool for many people in academic settings, sporting settings and trade related skills. Relying on quantity of practice alone may be detrimental in improving. A person may practice for 10 000 hours, but if they are practicing the wrong technique or practicing the skill with errors, they are becoming more proficient at the wrong thing or in the wrong way.

Quality of practice is very important. Regular assistance and receiving feedback are important. When a person can learn a skill with the assistance of an expert, or at least a very good teacher, it allows their quality of practice to improve. The expert or teacher can assist the person in improving in specific areas relevant to their goal, whilst also allowing for the individual's differences. Differences in a person's learning needs and strengths, their ability starting point regarding their learning goal, and their motivation are all relevant areas that once understood, can be used to improve a person's quality. The next aspect of quality practice is "deliberate practice". Deliberate practice can be defined as – practicing with the intent to be better. This often includes following advice from experts, and intentionally pushing oneself out of their comfort zone towards the desired goal. Some research including a meta-analysis from Brooke Macnamara and colleagues, found that deliberate practice can account for up to 26percent of skill variation. This suggests there are many other factors in a person becoming great.

One factor is the age at which a person begins the skill or technique. Research from Burgoyone and colleagues found that people who began practicing chess at a younger age, reached higher levels of skill then those who started in adulthood, even when accounting for deliberate practice.

As well as age, genetics has been found to be an important aspect when working towards greatness. However, as genetics is difficult to accurately use as a defining variable, most research uses twin studies. One such study used 15 000 twins (maternal and fraternal) in a drawing related experiment. The study found that there was a high correlation in skill level with the identical (maternal) twins compared to the fraternal twins. This makes sense as maternal twins often share 99percent of their genetics. Another study found that over 50percent of the variation between skilled readers and unskilled readers were found to be due to genetics. A study in Sweden tested more than 10 000 twins on their basic music abilities in relation to how much they had practiced. Their study found genes influenced approximately 38percent of the musical abilities measured with minimal evidence being found that the amount of practice in the young people influenced the difference in ability (compared to the identical twin that hadn't practiced). Regarding chess ability, there was a large variance in the time it took to reach a 'Chess Master' level of up to 22 times difference.

Other factors that influence the ability to become great at a skill include emotions, mental practice, and value behind the goal, which are discussed elsewhere in this book.

Quality combined with quantity may lead to a person becoming "great" at the chosen skill or technique, should their effort and motivation hold for the duration of their journey. A person may require approximately 728 hours of efficient quality practice, or they may require up to 16 120 hours of efficient quality practice. Not everyone wants to or needs to be great at something, and many people are happy practicing a skill or technique for fun or are happy understanding the basics.

Greene's Mastery

Greene discussed core aspects most people who had obtained greatness in their respective fields had in common – 'Primal Curiosity', 'Learning above all else' and 'Gathering Skills and Combining Skills in a Unique Way'. Primal Curiosity is the innate and individual curiosity that drives a person to want to improve and learn regarding a particular topic or field. Primal Curiosity includes "discovering your life's task", meaning what were the things that meant the most to you as a child and how can you pursue this as an adult. Greene suggests that regular journaling about what the person naturally found interesting when they were young, before they felt the external pressure to conform, can assist an adult in rediscovering their 'Primal Curiosity'.

Greene discussed that 'Learning above all else' is an important and often difficult step that many people who achieved greatness in their field took in their journey. Placing learning first can sometimes include accepting lower pay or reimbursement, receiving no recognition for efforts, facing harsh criticism, or implementing many hours of tedious practice and work. Placing learning first is also known as 'Prime Learning Opportunities', and this can sometimes include having to change most other aspects of your life to learn from the best people or organisations.

Some examples can include early career comedians or actors who often have to move to geographic locations they can't financially afford through to Muay Thai fighters who sleep on concrete for many years so that they can learn from the best coaches in Thailand. It can also include taking on unpaid or unofficial apprenticeships in the area you want to improve in and then working with a mentor that can assist your growth. Finally, this aspect also includes developing or honing your social intelligence. For some people this comes more naturally, whilst for others it is a skill that needs to be practiced. For your learning to assist in your longer-term financial future, a person needs to be able to communicate their knowledge in a way that is understood and eventually appreciated by other people. 'Learning above all else' is about the transformation of the person's mind and character, above all other ideas or rewards.

'Gathering Skills and Combining Skills in a Unique Way' is as the name implies, the act of gathering all relevant information and skills learnt and combining them in a way that is unique to the individual. When a person can combine their higher levels of skills and knowledge in a unique way, it often leads to a new idea, product or in some cases, unique fields of work and study. The combination of a person unlocking their own unique creative way of thinking allows the person to be able to combine the knowledge and their intuition in a way that allows for even better communication and understanding of your knowledge or skill.

Greatness Summarised

Becoming proficient in any task or knowledge is often enough. However, if a person strives for greatness in a chosen field or skill, hard work will always be a key component. Whether a person must practice or study for 700 hours or for 10 000 hours, their quality of study, and the relevant sacrifices they make to achieve their goal of greatness will strongly influence the outcome.

Notes:

Physics and Psychology

In my counselling practice, I often try to incorporate different areas, that I have learnt from informal science study to the various human body studies I have completed. Two areas often rarely combined are physics and psychology.

Physics concepts such as JND (Just Noticeable Difference) are relevant when discussing goal setting, motivation and stages of change models, but physics can also inform how a person learns. When taking a more wholistic health approach in psychology, physics concepts such as Wolff's law can be relevant to arthritis, nutrition and exercise discussions. Finally, when discussing social connection to people who are either very scientific or to people who are very spiritual in their life approach the physics idea of quantum entanglement theory can be used to discuss connection. Quantum entanglement theory briefly discusses that "things" are connected by energy, and many spiritual beliefs discuss that people are connected by energy.

Physics focuses on the structure of matter and its interactions between fundamental parts of the observable universe, and psychology focuses on the mental processes and behaviour in humans and animals. At the macro level these can be seen as very different areas of study however, at the micro and social levels these two areas of study and learning share many similarities.

The first area of learning positively impacted by both physics and psychology is known as the scientific method. When learning factual information, it is useful to understand the process behind how the information is gathered and what makes it a fact. This process is known as the scientific method.

The scientific method involves careful observation coupled with rigorous scepticism, because a person's cognitive assumptions can distort their interpretation of the observation. Scientific inquiry includes creating a hypothesis through inductive reasoning (a method of drawing conclusions by going from the specific to the general), testing it through experiments and statistical analysis, and adjusting or discarding the hypothesis based on the results. A scientific hypothesis must be falsifiable, implying that it is possible to identify a possible outcome of an experiment or observation that conflicts with predictions deduced from the hypothesis; otherwise, the hypothesis cannot be meaningfully tested. The purpose of an experiment is to determine whether observations agree or disagree with hypothesis.

The eight principles of the Scientific Method include – defining a question, gathering information and resources (observing), forming an explanatory hypothesis, testing the hypothesis by performing an experiment and collecting data in a reproducible manner, analysing the data, interpreting the data and drawing conclusions that serve as a starting point for a new hypothesis, publish results and lastly having the information retested (often completed by other scientists). In psychology this scientific model is used in research, procedural implementation, group program design and even in counselling. The only difference in psychology counselling the scientific model, is the person being seen by the professional would be represented as $N=1$, and the various psychological theories and tools would therefore have to be customised for effective counselling assistance.

The second area includes the relationship between an established theory of physics known as supersymmetry and a less recognised theory known as asymmetry-induced symmetry. In non-physics language, there are instances in which the observed behaviour of the system can be symmetric only when the system itself is not. This can also be explained as the microlevel being asymmetrical which then leads to the observable (macrolevel) becoming symmetrical. In psychology there is a similar idea where the individual is always different to everyone else, but at the macro level (society, town, culture, etc.) the differences or "chaos" averages out to behaviours known as socially acceptable or common behaviours.

This psychology and physics overlap is also useful in a learning environment. Every person has a different way of learning and retaining information (microlevel). However, despite schools and teachers trying their best to individualise education, they still have to use macrolevel education standards and tools.

Notes:

Change is a Direction & Not a Destination

According to the research from various sources, behavioural change can occur from 15-250 days. This is a large number variance and is the culmination of various sources being combined. Change involves a lot of hard work, time and consistency, and these elements lead to brain pathway changes, that then allow for future change. The key for many people is to improve their life a small amount on a regular basis, therefore assisting the person to make a change. Hence the title of this section – "Change is a Direction and not a Destination".

Whenever we have a thought, or practice a behaviour, the relevant neurological pathway in the brain is strengthened. Since the brain's main jobs are to keep us alive and be efficient, the brain will utilise the largest pathways possible for any thought or behaviour. The strengthening of the pathways often happens without us choosing as an adaptive efficiency response. This efficiency response is often a good thing as it allows a person to learn new behaviours or skills and can free up conscious thought for other tasks. The downside of these pathways happening autonomously is that if a person is practicing an unhealthy behaviour the pathways continue to increase and become more efficient with that specific behaviour. This is a neurological reason why behaviour change is difficult for many people. One way of being able to influence the brain's natural pathway response is to form healthy habits by choice.

Some research has reported that building habits can be separated into two phases – Defining and Designing Future Outcomes and Leveraging Your Subconscious. Defining and Designing Future Outcomes includes Defining the Objective and then Designing the Routine. Defining the Objective is used to understand what the overall goal is, such as "being fit" or "learning Spanish". During this part, the person needs to clearly understand why the overall goal is important and it often helps to write both the goal and the reason why it is important down. Designing the Routine involves breaking down the large goal into smaller and manageable steps (many of the goal frameworks discussed in this book can be helpful for this step).

The second phase known as Leveraging Your Subconscious has three aspects – The Start Button, Revisiting the Context & Repeating Actions and Enjoyable by Association. The

Start Button is where the person defines a clear trigger mechanism for the routine. This can include a visual pointer such as seeing a specific object, the time of day, workout clothing only being used for working out, etc., and is used to help create the context for your brain to do the behaviour. Revisiting the Context & Repeating Actions is where the person tries to change the brain pathway in their favour. The person uses the Start Button in the Context as regularly as possible. Lastly, associating the habit behaviour with other desirable activities can utilise the Enjoyable by Association idea. This can include listening to your favourite music while working out or using your favourite scent while cleaning.

Change is a direction and not a destination. Making small steps every day towards the larger goal can help form healthy habits and behaviours. Also, aiming for an 80percent compliance with the habit and behaviour in the correct direction allows for natural life events to happen without any negative self-judgement being associated with a perceived failure.

Notes:

Other Learning & Achieving Frameworks

Brief Introduction

There are various models and frameworks of learning discussed in psychology and in other fields such as education, sports coaching, teaching, etc. Different coaching frameworks such as AMN Academy and White Tiger Qigong have developed their own tools regarding how to learn a behaviour, both of which I use in my psychological practice. This section will discuss various learning frameworks often not directly focused on in psychology, but which can still benefit people individually and professionally.

Aboriginal 8 Pedagogy Framework

Here I will provide a brief overview of a learning style developed by First Nations People of Australia in collaboration with various education centres. During the process of writing this section, I requested assistance from one of my previous psychology supervisors that identifies as an Indigenous Australian. This was done to check for cultural appropriateness, as I wanted to include this learning framework as it provided a slightly different perspective and has aspects that many people could benefit from.

Aboriginal and non-Aboriginal teachers continue to contribute to the framework in an ongoing cross-cultural dialogue. It is managed by the Aboriginal Education Team at the Bangamalanha Centre (in New South Wales) and is a culturally safe point of entry for teachers to begin engaging with Aboriginal knowledge and cross-cultural dialogue in the community. Research from Louth and colleagues found that four dimensions of empowerment relating to embedding the Aboriginal and Torres Strait Islander perspectives of knowledge, understanding, perceptions and attitudes all increased for the teachers who completed training in the 8 Ways Aboriginal Pedagogical Framework. The Framework allows teachers to include Aboriginal perspectives by using Aboriginal learning techniques. In this way, focus can remain on core curriculum content while embedding Aboriginal perspectives in every lesson. It came from a research project involving DET staff, James Cook University's School of Indigenous Studies, and the Western New South Wales Regional Aboriginal Education Team between 2007 and 2009.

The Aboriginal Pedagogy Framework consists of eight interconnected pedagogies involving Narrative-Driven Learning (Story Sharing), Visualised Learning Processes (Learning Maps), Hands-on/Reflective techniques (Non-verbal), use of Symbols/Metaphors, Land-based Learning (Land Links), Indirect/Synergistic Logic (Non-Linear learning), Modelled/Scaffolded Genre Mastery (Deconstruct/Reconstruct), and Connectedness to Community. However, it is noted that these can adapt to the changing setting and are considered fluid and dynamic, resulting in a strong overlap across the eight areas. The 8 simple pedagogies are merely a starting point for dialogue and should not be considered a framework in the same way as the other frameworks discussed in this book.

Narrative-Driven Learning also known as Story Sharing is assisting the teacher and student to learn through story telling (yarning) instead of the concrete structure often taught in westernised education centres. The story sharing allows lessons to be taught whilst also allowing for the Indigenous Australian language experience to be demonstrated and shared. The story sharing also allows for the ethics, values, storied experiences, cultural meaning-making, place-based significance to be used to improve memory and cognition. Teachers and students are encouraged to share relevant personal stories with each other to help enrich the education material taught to the students whilst also building rapport and trust.

Visualised Learning Processes also known as Learning Maps is used to explicitly map and visualise ideas. The framework suggests that this allows for the Aboriginal intellectual processes to be visualised with the assistance of metaphors grounded in culture and country. Land-based Learning including the relevant Land Links are the dynamic set of relationships that contain vast schematics, knowledge system and intellectual processes that can be used to guide and enrich school systems and curricula. Hands-on/Reflective techniques also known as Non-verbal learning allows for the Aboriginal ways of relating and connecting to knowledge reflectively, critically, ancestrally, and physically. This is also known as seeing, thinking, acting, making, and sharing without words.

Symbols and Metaphors based learning is now becoming understood as a type of visual metalanguage which can be considered the building blocks for memory and the making of meaning, which is cross-cultural and dynamic. Visual images and metaphors can be created orally allowing for a deeper learning experience. Indirect/Synergistic Logic also known as Non-Linear learning is the cultural innovation through the interaction of cultural systems. This can be considered a way of approaching higher order thinking by laterally incorporating seemingly unrelated domains to create complex, real-life problems to be solved by learners using holistic thinking and innovative processes. Modelled/Scaffolded Genre Mastery also known as Deconstruct/Reconstruct learning engages with whole processes and texts, modelling and building upon a person's basic skills and identities and then transferring these successfully from familiar to unfamiliar contexts. This idea can also be thought as the ability to transfer knowledge and skills across forms and contexts.

Connectedness to Community is an important aspect of learning for many Indigenous Australians. The Community Link is the centrality of these relationships to the development and acquisition of all knowledge and highlights the importance of not just knowledge but rapport and cultural relationship. This also highlights the cultural importance of having the right people deliver the information, which is often not considered in the western education system.

It is strongly recommended that anyone wanting to implement this framework after completing the official training, follow some of the following ideas – work with community to identify the local Aboriginal systems in country and culture, explore the values inherent in the local culture, respect any local enduring protocols and, follow any reported processes that are locally used to inform the ways of interacting with changing social and ecological landscapes.

Notes:

Goal related frameworks

In modern times, goal frameworks often arise from corporate or group learning principles. The frameworks are often used to help a team or business to work towards a shared understanding or target. Many ideas discussed in these frameworks are beneficial for individuals as they may assist the individual in structuring their own personal or professional goals. When employees don't know one another's goals, they are more likely to make unrealistic demands, focus on activities that don't support their colleagues, or duplicate effort.

The ideas of recorded formalised goal setting dates to the ancient Greek philosopher Aristotle who developed his own version of goal setting known as the 'Four Causes'. When assessing today's modern goal theories, there are four common moderators - Ability, Task Complexity, Performance Feedback and Goal Commitment – which all affect us and our outcomes very differently. Goal setting is a theory of motivation that helps to explain what drives us all to perform better and achieve more than others. In more modern times formalised goal setting was formerly introduced by Bloom and colleagues in 1956 in their now famous work 'Taxonomy of Educational Objectives'. Many attribute the various goal frameworks to this work. As well as Bloom, there have been various other influential people such as Peter Druker in the 1950's, Edward Locke in the 1960's, Marcell Telles in the 1980's, as well as various other educators and even spiritual leaders. Finding the correct fit for an individual or team can be difficult, and often elements of goal templates are adapted into work and school settings.

For many the idea of a goal is simultaneously attractive and daunting, and in 2014 a study completed by Shafique, and colleagues found that of the people surveyed, 74 percent had failed in reaching their new year's resolution goals. In a psychology setting similar numbers are seen at the individual level, where people set goals and then fail to achieve them. One of the more common reasons for a person failing to achieve their goal, is a lack of clarity around what their goal means in real practical terms, and a lack of measurability regarding their progress. Whilst there are many variations of goal frameworks the ones discussed in this book include – the Bloom Taxonomy and the acronym frameworks – SMART, FAST, PACT, CLEAR, WOOP, WISE, and CLARITY.

Bloom Taxonomy

Bloom's Taxonomy is recommended as a teaching guide, more than an individual's goal setting tool. According to Forehand and colleagues there are several benefits to using Bloom's Taxonomy or the more recent revised Taxonomy. Firstly, it assists with establishing effective learning objectives so that teachers and students have a similar understanding of the purpose they are trying to achieve. Next it can assist in organising objectives and help clarify objectives for the teachers and students. And finally, it can assist in establishing an organised set of objectives to help teachers plan and deliver appropriate instruction, design valid assessment tasks and strategies, and ensure that instruction and assessment are aligned with the objectives.

The original Taxonomy included six different categories – Knowledge, Comprehension, Application, Analysis, Synthesis and Evaluation. Knowledge involved the recall of specific information and universally known information, the recall of methods and processes, or the recall of a pattern, structure or setting. Comprehension involved the understanding or apprehension of what is being communicated and the ability to make use of the material or idea being communicated without necessarily relating it to other material or seeing its fullest implications. Application involved the use of abstractions in specific and concrete situations. Analysis involved the breakdown of a communication into its constituent elements or parts, so that the usual hierarchy of ideas is made clear and the relations between ideas expressed is made explicit. Synthesis involved the combining of elements and parts so that they formed a whole. Finally, Evaluation involved the judgement about the value of material and methods for the given purposes.

This original Taxonomy had a massive influence in business and education and in 2001 the Taxonomy was revised following a lot of work from cognitive psychologists, curriculum theorists, instructional researchers and testing and assessment specialists. This new Taxonomy was more fluid and dynamic, as the experts believed that the original was too static for current use. The new Taxonomy made use of six aspects and could be explained using a pyramid structure with the first aspect 'Remember' being at the bottom, and 'Create' at the top of the pyramid. The six aspects are – Remember, Understand, Apply, Analyse,

Evaluate and Create. 'Remember' sits at the base of the Taxonomy pyramid and involves the ability to retrieve, recall, or recognise relevant knowledge from the long-term memory (such as recalling dates). 'Understand' is the second from the base of the Taxonomy pyramid and involves the ability to demonstrate the comprehension through one or more forms of explanation including comparison and definition. 'Apply' is the third from the base of the Taxonomy pyramid and involves the use of information or a skill in new situations. 'Analyse' is the third from the top of the Taxonomy pyramid and involves the ability to separate and breakdown information into its constituent parts and determine how the parts relate to each other or to an overall structure. 'Evaluate' is the second from the top of the Taxonomy pyramid and involves the ability to make judgements based on criteria and standards. Finally, 'Create' is the top of the Taxonomy pyramid and involves the ability to put elements together to form a new coherent or functional whole or reorganise elements into a new pattern or structure.

Following the success of the revised Taxonomy, some professionals wrote a version with a heavier focus on the types of knowledge used in cognition. The four knowledge types included Factual Knowledge, Conceptual Knowledge, Procedural Knowledge, and Metacognitive Knowledge. Factual Knowledge focused on terminology knowledge and the specific details and elements. Conceptual Knowledge focused on knowledge of classifications and categories, principles and generalisations, and theories, models, and structures. Procedural Knowledge focused on the knowledge of subject-specific skills and algorithms, subject-specific techniques and methods and the knowledge of criteria for determining when to use the most appropriate procedures. Finally Metacognitive Knowledge focused on strategic knowledge, knowledge about cognitive tasks including appropriate contextual and conditional knowledge and self-knowledge.

Another idea that was strongly influenced by the revised Taxonomy is Anderson's '25 Alternatives'. This version can also be seen as a supplementary framework to the revised Taxonomy. Here Anderson and colleague broke down thinking and goal setting into three levels of thinking order, with the Lower Order being for remembering, The Middle Order for Analysing, Applying and Understanding and the Higher Order thinking for Creating and Evaluating. In the Lower Order, Anderson included the following – Silence,

Speed/Tone/Volume changes, Signposting, Rhetorical Questions, Questions to Students, Redundances, Class Structure Repetition, Lying, Music relating to content, Videos relating to content, Theatre explanations and the listening to the Invited Speaker. In the Middle Order thinking, Anderson included – Moodle/Academic Tests, Online Contests, Incomplete Presentations and Interactive Activities. In the High Order level, Anderson included – Practical Group Exercises, Practical Individual Exercises, Class Debates, Thinking/Pairing/Sharing, Projecting Basic Learning, Challenge Based Learning, Inverted Classes and Improvised Classes.

The various versions of the Taxonomy were found to be useful in academic settings and for occupational psychology work, and less useful for the individual's goal setting. The following goal frameworks have various purposes, with some being better suited for individual and some better suited for groups.

SMART goals (Specific Measurable Achievable Realistic Timely)

The idea of SMART goals arose in 1981 from Doran and his colleagues who suggested that there was a better way to write goals and they developed the groundwork for today's SMART goals. SMART goals are a basic and structured template that can assist people in understanding how to achieve an end goal. Another interpretation is that SMART goals allow a person to understand their first step in a way that provides a clear understanding and responsibility of the outcome, on their way to achieving their desired result. As people are not robots, aiming for 100percent compliance with a SMART goal can be unrealistic, and some research suggests aiming for 80percent compliance.

The S in SMART stands for 'Specific' and SMART goal practitioners believe that goals should be specific enough that the individual and other people can understand what is trying to be achieved. Several prompts can be helpful in this section including – What the individual or team wants to achieve, Who needs to be involved to accomplish the goal, When does the goal need to be completed by and why should the goal be achieved in this exact way.

The M in SMART stands for 'Measurable' and SMART goal practitioners believe that goals should be able to be measured in a clear and precise manner. Understanding how to measure progress and success are important in achieving the goal but also for people as motivation and responsibility. Even if a goal is unsuccessful, if it was measured clearly, the individual or team can understand how and why they failed, which can lead to future improvement.

The A in SMART stands for 'Achievable' and SMART goal practitioners believe that goals should be achievable so that people understand their efforts will mean something. Prompts can be helpful such as – is the individual or team capable of achieving the goal, does everyone involved have the needed skills, and if they don't how can these skills be learnt or developed.

The R in SMART stands for 'Relevant' and SMART goal practitioners believe that goals should be understood clearly that any redundancy can be removed earlier in the process. Understanding the 'why' can help people understand why they want to achieve a goal and what the impact of their efforts leads to.

The T in SMART stands for 'Timely' and SMART goal practitioners believe that goals should have an end date. The end date allows for people to measure their progress, provides motivation and can help in assessing the other four aspects of the SMART goal regarding achievement.

A learning example of a SMART goal is – to read five pages, every day, for sixty days. If the goal is to read one 120-page book, then breaking the book down into a number of pages would be the simplest way to demonstrate the smart goal. The page number is Specific, Measurable, Achievable and Relevant, and the number of days is Timed.

SMART goals are best suited for helping a person identify specifics within their large goal and providing the person with steps to direct them and help them start.

FAST goals (Frequent Ambitious Specific Transparent)

The idea of FAST goals arose because business leaders such as Peter Druker felt that the previous approach to business goals were having a negative impact. One of the barriers to organisations using FAST goals is the fear of transparency. However, an analysis completed by Sull & Sull, found that of the companies that opted for this approach, almost 90percent of employees supported transparency for majority of their work-related goals. They also found that the structure allowed for teams and individuals to improve their performance up to the 80th percentile. The process and outcome of linking goals to measurable results, can often lead to greater value for the people involved in the task once it is completed.

The F in FAST stands for 'Frequently discussed' and FAST goal practitioners believe that goals should be embedded in ongoing discussions to allow for progress, resources, initiatives, and feedback to be assessed and improved. This approach can be helpful as it provides guidance for important decision making, assists in keeping teams focused on what matters most to the group, can link performance feedback to help concrete goals and can be used to evaluate progress and provide correction as needed.

The A stands for Ambitions and FAST goal practitioners believe that goals should be difficult but not impossible to achieve. This is thought to boost performance of the individual and the team, minimise the risk of plateauing and can assist in encouraging innovation.

The S stands for Specific and FAST goal practitioners believe that goals should be translated into measurable concrete metrics that encourage clarity, how the goal will be achieved, and progress measured. The benefits of this are that team members know what is expected of them, it helps to identify what is not working so it can be corrected and may encourage better performance from individuals and the team.

The T stands for Transparent and FAST goal practitioners believe that goals should be made public for all the team to see. This may allow peer pressure to become a motivator, helps individuals to understand the difference they are making, understand other team members' agendas and efforts and highlight redundant or unaligned strategies.

A learning example of a FAST goal is – finish a group project, one week prior to its due date, and edit using a group accessible cloud drive, with all members completing one section each. The group project would require Frequent Discussion regarding information, direction, etc. Finishing it early would be Ambitious as deadlines in formal learning environments and workplaces are often already difficult to meet. The dividing of the project into sections allows for the Specific aspect of FAST to be met. And the use of a cloud drive allows for Transparency.

FAST goals are best suited for tasks or projects that involve multiple people.

PACT goals (Purposeful Actionable Continuous Trackable)

The history of PACT goals is unclear; however, some business professionals believe the focus of PACT is more conducive to achieving company goals than SMART goals. The PACT approach focuses on the output instead of a specific outcome. It's about continuous growth rather than the pursuit of a well-defined achievement. PACT goals are also thought to work well for neurodivergent people such as ADHD instead of the traditional SMART goal approach.

The P in Pact stands for 'Purposeful' and PACT goal practitioners believe that goals should be meaningful to a longer-term purpose in life. This approach can be helpful because when a goal has value or purpose it assists with internal motivation, motivation to improve, and or achieve.

The A in Pact stands for 'Actionable' and PACT goal practitioners believe that goals should be controllable and actionable. This approach can be helpful as it assists in shifting a person's mindset from longer-term outcomes in the future to present outputs the person can control. It also helps in making the person feel their desired learning outcome is within reach, acting today rather than overplanning for tomorrow.

The C in Pact stands for 'Continuous' and PACT goal practitioners believe that goals should be simple, flexible and repeatable. This approach can be helpful as it can lessen the choice paralysis that many people experience from having too many possibilities or choices. Once the person starts, they begin to learn more, which allows for adaptation as they work towards their learning goal. The idea is that continuous improvement may be less daunting to people compared to a specific outcome.

The T in Pact stands for 'Trackable' and PACT goal practitioners believe that goals should be trackable instead of measurable. This approach can be helpful as tracking the progress can be done more simply with such as "yes or no" type questions, instead of specific data sets that can lead to procrastination or be misleading. The "yes or no" approach makes it easier for the individual and other people in a team setting to see if progress is being made and if steps are being completed.

An example of a PACT goal might be a person's life mission statement and is often strongly influenced by a person's own value systems.

CLEAR goals (Collaborative Limited Emotional Appreciable Refinable)

CLEAR goals were introduced by Locke and colleagues during the 1980's and were developed for group goals where collaboration is focus and is often used in the workplace or volunteer organisation but can be effective with most group activities.

The C in CLEAR stands for 'Collaborative'. CLEAR goal practitioners believe that goals should involve buy-in from individual members of the group and that all group members should understand the common goal and the process in how to get there.

The L in CLEAR stands for 'Limited'. CLEAR goal practitioners believe that goals should have time and financial boundaries, and that all members should understand what this looks like. Understanding these boundaries is thought to improve the goal being achieved.

The E in CLEAR stands for 'Emotional'. CLEAR goal practitioners believe that goals should have emotional investment from all members. This is thought to assist in providing motivation during the more difficult periods.

The A in CLEAR stands for 'Appreciable', meaning measurable. CLEAR goal practitioners believe that goals should be able to be measured in a way that suits all members of the group, so that progress can be monitored, and so that all members can be held accountable.

The R in CLEAR stands for 'Refinable'. CLEAR goal practitioners believe that goals should allow for adjustments to be made during the process of working towards the goal. This also allows for changes in circumstances, whilst also allowing for continued input from the group members.

A learning example of a CLEAR goal is – Save $5000 by end of April for a family holiday to Western Australia. The family holiday allows for the emotional investment, the money amount is the appreciable/measurable figure, and the location can be refined/changed if need be.

WOOP goals (Wish Outcome Obstacle Plan)

WOOP goals were first introduced by Oettingen and colleagues as an alternative to the SMART goal framework. It was originally designed for younger people but has been found to be effective for anyone who tends to self-sabotage. This suggests that it may be more helpful than other goal frameworks for people with depression, anxiety, and other mental health difficulties.

The W in WOOP stands for 'Wish' and WOOP goal practitioners believe that goals should allow for challenge and change without whelming oneself. It can be used as a slower, kinder approach.

The O in WOOP stands for 'Outcome'. WOOP goal practitioners believe that goals should assist the person in identifying the best possible outcome, such as a smaller attainable goal or a larger more challenging but still realistic goal.

The second O in WOOP stands for 'Obstacle'. WOOP goal practitioners believe that goals should also allow the person to identify any obstacles that may hinder progress or success, and these can include "real" meaning external obstacles such as other people, finances, or tasks, or can include "imagined" meaning internal barriers such as self-image, confusion, etc.

The P in WOOP stands for 'Plan'. WOOP goal practitioners believe that goals should assist a person in tracking their habits such as a journal, allow for self-care, and allow for smaller goals such as micro-goals to be achieved on a regular basis.

A 'WOOP' goal is designed to help a person manage their inner difficulties to lessen the behaviours associated with their prior self-sabotage.

> *WISE goals* (Written Integrated Synergistic Expansive)

WISE goals were introduced to assist a person who is setting multiple goals, to more effectively plan their goals to work together or assist each other, instead of the goals hindering each other.

The W in WISE stands for 'Written'. WISE goal practitioners believe that goals should be written down on paper or digitally to allow the person to work towards multiple goals whilst minimising confusion.

The I in WISE stands for 'Integrated'. WISE goal practitioners believe that goals should fit together in some way. This might include time, travel, or any other common element.

The S in WISE stands for 'Synergistic'. WISE goal practitioners believe that goals should be working in the same direction. It is difficult to save money, if a person also has a goal to pay off a debt simultaneously.

The E in WISE stands for 'Expansive'. WISE goal practitioners believe that goals should challenge oneself enough that it motivates the person. The challenge should be a motivator and not lead to whelming oneself. 'Expansive' is a flexible part of the 'WISE' model and should adapt to allow for goals to be met efficiently as possible.

A learning example of a WISE goal is – to pay off all debts including a car and house within 10-15 years, without negatively impacting the family's mental health.

Goal Summary

All goal frameworks have beneficial ideas, and most practitioners of a particular goal framework feel that their choice is the better one for their needs. It is up to the individual to identify if any of the current frameworks are beneficial, or if there are ideas in each of them, they can benefit from. Using any formal goal framework can assist in learning more efficiently and either achieving or understanding a failure more easily. Using a goal framework also assists by giving the relevant person or group responsibility over the outcome as well as clarity and direction.

Notes:

Types of intelligence IQ/EQ/AQ

The idea of intelligence is controversial and ever changing. I use the idea of different types of intelligence when helping a person identify their areas of strength, especially when their strengths don't meet the traditional academic idea of intelligence.

There are theorised to be at least nine types of IQ (Intelligence Quotient) intelligence which can be an influential factor when people are trying to learn. The nine types are Spatial, Naturalist, Musical, Logic/Mathematical, Existential, Interpersonal, Bodily/Kinaesthetic, Linguistic, and Intrapersonal.

Spatial intelligence often refers to a person's ability to generate, retain, retrieve, and transform well-structured visual images. This can include visualising the outcome such as sculpting or geometry and can also include the ability to understand sizes and spaces without the assistance of measuring devices.

Naturalist intelligence often refers to a person's ability to identify, classify and manipulate elements of the environment, objects, animals, or plants leading to our ability to recognise differences between species and understand how they relate to each other.

Musical intelligence often refers to a person's ability to perceive, distinguish, transform, and express sounds and musical forms. It allows people to create, communicate and understand meaning through sound. This intelligence includes sensitivity to the rhythms, melodies, and tones of a piece of music.

Logic/Mathematical intelligence often refers to a person's ability of scientific reasoning, mathematical calculation, logical thinking, inductive and deductive reasoning, and the sharpness of abstract patterns and relationships. The five traits of mathematical logic are classification, comparing, mathematical operations, inductive and deductive reasoning, and the forming and rechecking of hypotheses. This area of intelligence is often paired with a person's numeracy ability, which refers to the person's ability to use numbers and mathematical concepts in everyday life, such as connections with the mathematical concepts of fractions and addition to a recipe.

Bodily/Kinaesthetic intelligence often refers to a person's ability to manipulate objects and use a variety of physical skills. This intelligence also involves a sense of timing and the perfection of skills through mind–body union. Athletes, dancers, surgeons, and crafts people exhibit well-developed bodily kinaesthetic intelligence. Linguistic intelligence often refers to a person's ability to think in words and to use language to express and appreciate complex meanings.

Linguistic intelligence allows us to understand the order and meaning of words and to apply meta-linguistic skills to reflect on our use of language. Linguistic intelligence is the most widely shared human competence and is evident in poets, novelists, journalists, and effective public speakers.

Existential intelligence often refers to a person's ability to tackle deep questions about human existence, such as the meaning of life, why we die, and how did we get here and often includes spiritual leaders and philosophers.

Interpersonal intelligence often refers to a person's ability to understand and interact effectively with others. It involves effective verbal and nonverbal communication, the ability to note distinctions among others, sensitivity to the moods and temperaments of others, and the ability to entertain multiple perspectives. Teachers, actors, politicians, leaders, and charismatic people often exhibit interpersonal intelligence.

Intrapersonal intelligence often refers to a person's ability to understand oneself and one's thoughts and feelings, and to use such knowledge in planning and directing one's own life. Intra-personal intelligence involves not only an appreciation of the self, but also of the human condition. It is evident in psychologist, spiritual leaders, and philosophers. It is theorised that most people whose strengths include Interpersonal, Intrapersonal and/or Existential intelligence, often have a more developed emotional intelligence.

EQ (Emotional Quotient) also known as emotional intelligence is theorised to be an even stronger predictor or influencer regarding a person achieving the result of their goal. The five types of EQ are Self-Awareness, Self-Management, Motivation, Empathy and Social Skills. Self-Awareness can be briefly explained as a person's ability to understand their own emotions and intentions. Self-Management is the ability to manage one's own efforts and behaviours. Motivation is the ability to find internal and external reasons and use processes to direct oneself towards achieving their goals. Empathy is the ability to tune into and understand others' emotions and situations. Lastly, Social Skills is the ability to interact easily and healthily with other people, often seen as being extroverted and/or charismatic. The five types of EQ are very interactive and are rarely separated as they are in this book, and have strong interactions with the above Interpersonal, Intrapersonal and Existential Intelligence Quotients.

Finally, more recent research has highlighted AQ (Adaptive Quotient) as the most important indicator of success. This includes our ability to adapt and may also include the speed at which a person, team or organisation can adapt to change.

The benefits of a person having a high adaptability combined with a fast cognitive processing ability and skill can sometimes have a negative effect on a person's memory retention. One tool to manage this possible negative effect is mindful thinking. Mindful thinking involves a person paying attention to one thing, in the present moment and can involve repeating or paraphrasing information, writing information, or reorganising information as the person is learning it.

No type of intelligence is inherently superior, and all people have their own combination of the various interpretations of intelligence. What is more important is how a person is able to utilise their strengths, how the environment supports and allows the person's strengths to be used and the person's goals and values. When a person finds the "right fit" their strengths and values align with the school or organisation they are a part of.

Notes:

Defining motivation and "the Why"

As mentioned, many of the goal frameworks work on exploring the motivation behind learning at the group level. They discuss briefly how the group narrative influences the individual motivation to achieve an agreed upon goal. Here we will briefly look at the individual aspects of motivation, also known as "the Why". The various subsections all overlap and are rarely separated as they are in this book. They have been separated here for simplicity and clarity.

Motivation Types

There are three motivation types, Internal, External Positive and External Negative. Internal motivation is also known as inspiration and often leads to a person wanting to learn information or perform a task for their own internal interests or goals. When a person is interested, their internal motivation increases and their want to learn or perform a particular behaviour will increase. This is often a slight increase and can make setting up goals and other motivations easier. The difficulty of relying on internal motivation is that it is often short lived. This can lead to large improvements becoming less likely, because the person might give up, or wait until the next inspiration. Internal motivation is a great time to build structure and begin the goal, and if used correctly, can then be maintained by the other aspects of motivation.

Another type of motivation is known as external motivation. The two types of external motivation I discuss with clients include External Positive and External Negative Motivation. External Positive Motivation is when a person can use or be influenced by positive environmental motivators such as other people (in a team) or an upcoming holiday date. This type of motivation can be helpful in maintaining goals that had been set up during the inspiration stage and can be useful in the continued learning of difficult tasks. The various goal frameworks discussed earlier can be used as external positive motivation tools. External Negative motivation involves the external pressure or threat of an environmental stimulus or person as the motivator. Examples include bills, due dates, work performance indicators, etc. This type of motivator can be used as a beneficial tool, but if relied upon can lead to burnout, disinterest and various other negative emotional and physical responses to the task or information the person is trying to improve or complete.

When a person understands how to utilise the combination of Internal Motivation and External Motivation, it makes it easier for them to achieve their goals. The combination and specific motivators are often contextual and therefore should change or be adapted as such to improve the chances of success.

Notes:

3 Forgotten Motivation Areas

Three areas often forgotten when discussing motivation and learning are: Value Adding, Routine & Creativity, and Silliness & Fun.

Value Adding

When we value something enough, we often find time for the task or learning. How a person adds value can often be contextual and be strongly influenced by the person's own life experiences. A person's core value such as kindness can be a tool for adding value to a behaviour or learning, as can other examples including – the end goal, interest, pressure, and other powerful emotions such as hope.

Routine

A person's daily, learning and life routines can greatly assist or hinder progress in learning or achieving. A person's sleep and health routines can impact how well they are feeling physically and mentally which will then impact how much energy and motivation they have available for learning or improvement. A person's learning routine can impact how efficient and successful their time spent learning is (as discussed in the 'Illusion of learning' section). And a person's life routine, the behaviour they have maintained over a long period of time can greatly impact their ability to learn new information or tasks or improve on current ones. When a behaviour becomes a habit, the routine of this habit becomes its own motivator.

Creativity, Silliness and Fun

Creativity, silliness, and fun can mean the same thing or have different interpretations, but all can be used to assist in learning. Creativity can include thinking "outside the box" or can mean learning or expressing learnings and behaviours artistically. Adding silliness and fun to a task by reorganising the task can allow a person's brain to lessen the internal obstacles because of the stimulation and endorphins triggered by the silliness or fun aspect. This can include attempting to "moon walk" whilst brushing one's teeth or can be more interactive such as "ice break" activities often used in large team meetings or presentations.

Notes:

Identifying Obstacles

Part of understanding the motivation is also understanding any barriers, whether internal or external. Some barriers can be both internal and external obstacles such as language, culture, learning differences and age. At first, they seem to be induvial and therefore internal, but the social supports or lack of social supports can strongly influence whether these internal aspects become obstacles or not.

Internal Obstacles can include low self-image, stress, emotional triggers, perception of self, etc. Often our perception including our life history, own emotions and the context of the goal or learning objective influence how the person responds to the idea and the required behaviours. These all can all form part of our internal obstacles and can negatively interact with any external obstacles leading to a person feeling lost, defeated, whelmed, etc., before they even start their learning journey. Once a person understands what their internal obstacles are, they have an opportunity to process or overcome these (often with professional supports) prior to initiating their learning behaviour.

External Obstacles can often lead a person feeling powerless, helpless, and hopeless. Common examples of external obstacles can include institutional discrimination (including racism, gender discrimination and financial discrimination), cost of living, responsibilities such as children or bills, geographic location, language barriers and many others. Whilst identifying external obstacles can seem counter-productive to achieving any learning goals, it can also be helpful if done with the right intent. By identifying any external obstacles, a person is then able to plan ways to overcome these, which might then lead to their learning behaviours being more successful. For example, if a person identifies that a professional institution favours a specific type of professional qualification, they can either choose to study that specific qualification or choose a more supportive institution prior to beginning their learning behaviour.

Once a person has understood and developed processes or skills to overcome any identified obstacles, their learning journey will often be more successful. Suggestions to help with overcoming obstacles include – joining a study or relevant social group, changing institutions, or choosing a more supportive institution, seeking professional assistance such as speaking with a psychologist/careers counsellor/tutor and investing in self-care no matter the learning goal.

Notes:

Awareness of the Treacherous Trio

There are three common types of emotional filtering that impact a person's ability to learn and interact with other people: Confirmation Bias, Cognitive Dissonance and Motivated Reasoning. These three types of unhelpful thinking can severely impact a person's ability to learn and improve and interact with the world. There is a strong overlap across these three types of thinking, but I have tried to separate these as much as possible to assist a person in understanding them more effectively. Almost everyone has at least one, if not all three of these unhelpful thinking styles depending on the topic. This is because the human brain is developed to look for difference and similarity and is often socially and emotionally driven rather than logically driven. Despite how logical a person is, they will still have some version of social and emotional thinking that colours their opinions and worldview.

Confirmation Bias occurs when a person confirms their own viewpoint as more accurate than information that doesn't fit their viewpoint – "The Earth is flat because the horizon is flat". Cognitive Dissonance is the internal tension that occurs whenever a person holds two cognitions that are psychologically inconsistent – "The Earth is flat, but I accept ALL planets are spherical". Finally, Motivated Reasoning is the tendency to accept what we want to believe with much more ease and much less analysis than what we don't want to believe – "The majority of scientists lie about the earth being rounded, as there was one scientist who said the earth was flat". All three are similar and are used to explain how no-one sees the world how it is, but rather they perceive the world based on their own experiences, expectations, and belief systems.

When a person understands their Confirmation Bias, it can help them to lessen the impact of the bias, which in turn may allow them to improve their ability seek more accurate and relevant assistance in their learning journey. For example, if a person is aware that they have an age bias, they might then be willing to ask older people for assistance, once they have spent time and effort in overcoming this bias. This might also allow for incidental learning to occur as well as improving their social emotional connections and skills.

When a person understands their Cognitive Dissonance, it can help direct their planning phase of their learning to overcoming this internal obstacle. When a person understands why they hold the cognitive dissonance, they can spend energy and time reducing the dissonance and its impact.

Finally, when a person understands what causes their Motivated Reasoning, it allows them to develop more efficient learning plans for themselves or for people they teach or influence. For example, a teacher who uses a meta-analysis on learning in combination with one-on-one conversations with students and their parents, can then use this combination of qualitative and quantitative information to challenge their own beliefs regarding what teaching methods are best for learning difficulties.

We are all human, and we will all continue to have varying degrees of bias, dissonance, and motivated reasoning, however, being aware of our version of these, can lead to better individual outcomes for the individual, and for anyone they influence.

Notes:

Music, Sound, & learning

Music and sounds have been used for thousands of years to improve a person's health. In approximately the last 100 years many western science studies have examined if music and sounds could be utilised to improve a person's ability to learn. With the understanding of neuroscience and the invention of various brain modelling technologies (such as the fMRI and PET scans) and techniques, scientists have been able to study the impacts of sounds and music more directly.

Playing and Listening to Music

The brain processes language, sound, and the written word, and when done together activates multiple areas across the brain. Recent studies have demonstrated that music activates both the left and right brain hemispheres simultaneously. This can lead to improvements in learning and memory. The sound enters the ears and travels along the auditory pathway that interacts with other areas of the brain that impacts our movement, speech, thinking patterns, speech patterns, knowledge and memory retention and focus. Hearing engages our cognitive, sensory, motor and reward systems in the body, often simultaneously, and more so when the person is playing an instrument.

When a person is learning to play an instrument, their eye sees a symbol, their brain hears the sound and attaches or reinforces a memory to the music and speech sound, the brain instructs the body to make the specific sound, and then the brain listens and attunes to the sound. Some studies suggested that musicians' memory retrieval advantage can be explained by their brain's ability to give each memory multiple "trigger tags", where one memory can be associated with a conceptual tag, an emotional tag, an audio tag as well as a contextual tag. As well as this, some research has found that the brain can become up to 30 percent denser (this is a good thing) in students who learn to play instruments compared to those who don't learn. This greater density also has been found to improve overall brain efficiency, allowing the brain to have greater capacity for daily tasks and learning new information.

The brain's need for efficiency becomes a strength when learning material that has music attached to it, via the brain's pattern recognition ability. The brain looks for pattern in the sound and any information relevant to that pattern is stored more comprehensively, allowing for easier retrieval in the future. The pattern skill of the brain is improved through learning to play a musical instrument – reading sheet music teaches not just musical notation and the connection to the specific sound, but also activates a phonological loop leading to a deepening of sound-word connections. When the brain processes sound, it strengthens the same areas of the brain that are responsible for learning language and learning to read, suggesting that music and reading are complementary. Other ways in which learning a musical instrument can improve a person's language skills include separating speech from noise, improving aural perception, assisting in earlier language acquisition, improving hearing prosody in speech, improving a person's language syntax, learning unique words, improving phonological skills and improving language comprehension.

Learning to play a musical instrument has been found to train the brain in areas beyond learning the specific instrument. Some longitudinal studies have found that when people learnt a musical instrument as a younger child and continued this learning, they were much less likely to develop Alzheimer's or Dementia symptoms in older age. Music researchers such as Anita Collins found — if a person begins learning a musical instrument before the age of seven the minimum amount of time recommended before they can reap the long-term benefits in late adult hood is two years. This minimum becomes three years if the person begins after the age of seven for long term benefits, but the longer a person learns musical instruments, the greater the long-term benefits are regarding learning and music.

Some studies suggested that people who learnt an instrument instead of only listening to music, performed better at sporting and academic tasks than people who listened to music only. Some academic tasks not often linked to music that have improved by the person learning an instrument include — improved mathematical ability, improvement in planning and strategising ability, improved attention to detail and improved simultaneous analysis of both cognitive and emotional aspects of a problem or task. Other executive brain functioning benefits relating to learning a musical instrument include improving the level of attention and focus and assisting with strategy, planning and time management skills. Learning an instrument builds movement maps also known as muscle memory, which has been found to translate to improved body awareness in sports that utilise the same body areas – learning to play a double bass can assist a person in understanding their body, leading to improved muscle control, which can then assist in ball and bat sports due to the brain's mapping of the body. The improved mapping of the body also has been found to improve general fine motor skills required for daily tasks, with people who have played an instrument showing a slowed deterioration of fine motor skills in older age. Sport and music are complimentary to each other. Sport often includes competition which improves a person's ability to focus and shutout irrelevant stimuli, while music allows a person to absorb sensory stimuli in order to understand and differentiate, leading to a greater ability to understand one's internal and external environments. Learning a musical instrument has also been found to improve teamwork and spatial awareness.

There are various benefits of listening to music in learning, and some include emotional processing, focus improvement, destressing, etc. For example, music helps people to process their emotions by consciously choosing their favourite style of music and often subconsciously choosing the required beats per minute. The beats per minute combined with the chosen music style also helps to destress and relax the person. Some studies have found that the impact of listening to music can have similar effects on destressing as remedial massage, at least in the shorter-term. Janata and colleagues used Functional Magnetic Resonance Imaging (fMRI) and found that music assists in memory retrieval by triggering emotions relevant to the historic event, whether formal learning or life event.

The specific type of music does not matter as much as previously thought. Scientists previously thought that classical music was best for calming and high beats per minute music was best for energising. Whilst this is true for some people, there are many people who can have an opposite response to specific music. Rap music and heavy metal music often associated with aggression and energy, can assist some people in calming and focusing. Some studies have found that the style of music might have less impact on short-term focus but can impact how effectively the brain organises the new information.

Regarding formalised learning such as exam preparations, many recent studies have found that music assisted students in learning more material and retaining more information compared to people who did not use music during study preparation. Music has also been found to improve a person's reading ability by assisting with sound recognition which then leads to an improvement of recognising letter and word sounds and sound combinations. Music has had similar effects on sporting related learning such as basketball shooting, where people who listened to music while practicing three-point shooting, were found to have higher percentages compared to people who practiced without music.

Music also strengthens social skills including social connection. There are various examples with the most common examples of how music directly assists with social connection to people known and not known including – sporting anthems, Christmas carols, nursery rhymes and popular music choruses. Music therefore strengthens a person's social emotional learning, and as humans are a social species, this can assist many other areas of human learning. By improving a person's social connection, music can indirectly enhance other socio-emotional skills such as the ability to identify emotions internally and from other people and manage and express emotions constructively. Other social and emotional skill improvements that have been connected with learning a musical instrument include improving a person's overall wellbeing and their insight regarding their wellbeing, increasing positive social behaviours including healthier social engagement, improving non-verbal skills, improving empathy and improving a person's perceived personality (allowing for easier social interaction).

Playing a musical instrument can also increase the volume and activity in the brain's Corpus Callosum. The Corpus Callosum is known as the brain's bridge between the two hemispheres, and improvements in this area lead to better communication between the two brain hemispheres. This strengthening of the Corpus Callosum can then lead to improved emotion regulation, which can then improve a person's ability to calm or focus.

Boys's Music Engagement

This subsection will be drawing heavily from Anita Collins' and colleagues' research as well as various other sources that referenced her research.

Prior to the age of 13, the engagement in music from boys and girls is very similar. However, after the age of 13 (during the ages of 13 to 16 especially), the research demonstrated that in a large majority of schools in Australia and internationally, boys' participation in learning a musical instrument drastically decreased, and if a boy was to continue playing an instrument, it often changed to a gender stereotyped instrument. The research discussed that the primary causational reason for this change is a boy's environment.

There were multiple positive environmental aspects that increased male engagement in playing a musical instrument and these included – success and praise from male role models, regular accomplishment that is noticeable, positive parental support that didn't emphasise perceived gender stereotypes, access to technology and support to create their own music, sense of acceptance from other peers (especially other male peers), school culture regarding how music is discussed and received (and what instruments were taught) and an overall interactive learning environment. Individually the young male had to have an interest and positive attitude towards music, success and acceptance and praise, which could all be generated by the above positive environmental factors.

When the environment was supportive, didn't focus on perceived gender norms, was interactive and small successes were acknowledged or celebrated, the rates of boys' stopping engagement in playing a musical instrument drastically reduced, and in some schools the rates were able to increase.

Sound

New technology utilising sounds such as Audio Bilateral Stimulation (Audio BLS) and Audio Binaural Sounds have also been found to improve the brain's Corpus Callosum. The most basic version of audio BLS involves a basic sound going from one ear to the next. This basic audio BLS example is used in psychology to help a person calm their emotional brain centres and to help them focus, by activating the Corpus Callosum via sound. The Binaural Sound utilises a different approach to activate the Corpus Callosum. The Binaural Sound involves each ear receiving a different sound or sound frequency. The frequency difference between the waves entering the left and right ear that the person may perceive consciously or not helps the brain to calm and to focus. When a person's brain is calmer, the brain has an improved ability to access the frontal regions used in problem solving, learning and movement. These improvements have been measured with the use of electroencephalogram (EEG) in various studies, with similar results across the board.

Summary

As discussed, there are many ways in which music and sound can improve a person's overall health, learning ability and physical ability. There are too many studies to reference, but most have found music is positively correlated with increased performance across most aspects of life. The type of instrument learnt, the choice of listening music type and the beats per minute are all individual, but once the right fit can be found, it can become a long-term positive lift habit. During the ages 13 to 16 the male social brain is very vulnerable to environmental opinions. Knowing what we know about the benefits of playing a musical instrument and what it can offer a person's brain long-term, it is important that boys have the opportunity and encouragement to continue or start learning a musical instrument regardless of the specific instrument.

The more recent formalised types of sounds such as Audio Bilateral Stimulation and Binaural Sounds are yet another example and tool of how sound can improve a person's overall health and functioning.

Notes:

Neurodivergence & Learning – a basic discussion

Neurodivergence can simply be explained as 'brain difference'. This definition is very open and can be used for any person and is commonly used when discussing a person who has a diagnosable or diagnosed mental health difference, disorder, or illness. In this section I will be focusing more on how the Autistic (Diagnosed label known as Autism Spectrum Disorder/ASD), ADHD (Attention Deficit Hyperactivity Disorder) and Trauma brains may learn differently. There is also a growing body of research discussing the advantages of neurodivergence and how it has theoretically influenced and assisted in our societal and technology advancement.

Autism and ADHD learning brain

Brief Introduction

Everyone knows everyone is different, but there are also some further differences with the Autistic and ADHD brains. For example, neurotypical brains generally use stimulation as a tool to excite the brain. Whereas, for many Autistic and ADHD brains, stimulation can be a helpful tool for calming and focus, if the correct stimulation is used. This small section is only a summary and only lists some information and suggestions that many of my neurodivergent clients have found helpful over the years.

Research studies have found that 30-80percent of people who have been diagnosed ADHD would also meet the diagnostic threshold for ASD, and 20-50 percent of people who were diagnosed ASD would also meet the diagnostic threshold for ADHD. For simplicity most of this chapter will combine the ASD and ADHD learning differences, however, this section could be its own book with the amount of information now available.

Autism is a complex, neurological disorder characterised by deficits in communication and behaviour often seen as deficits in social-emotional skills. Some studies utilised an

EEG (electroencephalogram) and their results suggested that autistic children have deficits in the number of mirror neurons which might explain some of the development delays and some of the brain difference. Other common difficulties Autistic people may experience include poorer Interoception, Proprioception and Exteroception, greater need for Stimming, Relationship and Communication differences and a greater Emotional Intensity when triggered. Many people with diagnosed ASD are often encouraged to seek professional mental health assistance and can occasionally be prescribed mood stabilisers with mixed results. The most common difficulty faced by people who have been diagnosed ASD regarding seeking mental health assistance is not feeling heard or understood by neurotypical approaches and professionals.

ADHD is another common complex neurological disorder that is characterised by difficulties regarding – regulating attention, sense of time (also known as time blindness), planning and prioritising, working memory, meta-cognition, starting and shifting tasks, self-regulation and adapting to changes. Many ADHD adults are also encouraged to seek mental health assistance, alongside a prescribed medication. However, ADHD people also report that the most common difficulty regarding seeking mental health assistance is not feeling heard or understood by neurotypical approaches and professionals.

However, for many Autistic and ADHD people, the brain difference can become a strength once the individual and their support people understand how to use the brain difference as a strength. This approach doesn't undo any difficulties the person might have, rather helps the person to achieve their goals and live a better quality of life.

Differences and Strengths

When a person is interested in a topic, the brain often allows for more resources to be used, thereby making attempting, or completing the task easier. The same is true for the Autistic and ADHD brains, however, this is heightened and known as fixated thinking or hyperfocus.

The difference between fixated thinking, hyperfocus and being interested is the intensity at which the person experiences that interest. When a person is interested, their internal motivation increases and their want to learn or perform a particular behaviour also increases. This is often a slight increase and can make setting up goals and other motivations easier. Fixated thinking is more common with the neurodivergent brain and is when a person experiences a more intense interest about a behaviour, topic, or theme. This can be helpful as it allows for an even greater amount of internal motivation but can come at the cost of other areas of functioning, including daily functioning or social functioning. Fixated thinking often lasts many years, sometimes a lifetime and a person can experience fixated thinking in combination with hyperfocus. Both Fixated thinking and Hyperfocus can be known as being passionate about a topic or outcome.

Hyperfocus is the greatest of the three intensities and allows the person's ability, quality and/or quantity to be greater than their normal functioning. This is a strength, often called a superpower, as during hyperfocus the person initiate tasks, set up structure for goals and start multiple tasks or learn the basics for multiple topics at once. The weakness of hyperfocus is it is often short lived, often up to six months. This then leaves a person with multiple tasks started, with the person struggling to use any form of motivation or goal framework without external assistance, leading to feeling whelmed or burnout.

The Autistic and ADHD memory can also be different. Firstly, the discussed fixated thinking and hyperfocus, can assist in memory of information and of ability for the specific interest topics, during the interest period. However, daily memory functioning can be impacted negatively as well. The busy brain pays less attention to one task at a time, and this leads to the information or behaviour not being retained in memory.

There are many ideas that neurodivergent people can use to improve their memory retention and some include– choosing to focus for 5-10 seconds on the task, speaking the task or information out loud, adding association and value (such as movement, interest and motivations), writing the task, using adapted versions of power cards (often utilising a person's interest topic or character), slowing a task down to allow for more conscious attention on the task and the use of the 'Eisenhower Box'. The Eisenhower Box can be explained as a simple decision matrix that is used to help a person prioritise a task or list of tasks based on their urgency and importance. Another idea often practiced by neurodivergent people involves movement. Many neurodivergent people have reported that by combining movement when they learn, their ability to focus and remain calm increases. The research supports this idea further, by discussing that the use of the Proprioceptive and Vestibular systems in movement can promote focus in some people.

Recent neurodivergence related nutrition research has also found that nutrition and exercise play an important role in the regulation of endorphins and focus. The research has suggested that neurodivergent people benefit more than their neurotypical peers with higher levels of Proteins and Omegas and benefit more from exercise.

Notes:

Trauma brain learning differences

Trauma can be defined as "any event where a person feels helpless, hopeless and/or powerless", which can include direct abuse, vicarious trauma, neglect, or other forms. Trauma impacts a person's brain and body at multiple levels. Since this is about how trauma effects learning, I will be focusing more specially on the negative impacts of trauma that specifically impact a person's ability to learn. Trauma effects the entire body leading to multiple physical and psychological difficulties and disorders, discussed further in the book 'My Eclectic Human Body'.

When a person experiences trauma it can rewire their brain. When a person experiences trauma at a young age (pre-12 years of age) it can rewire their brain impacting not only focus, but also impacting – how and when endorphins are released, memory, emotional regulation, learning ability, the levels of cortisol and dopamine in the body that are available as well as impact a person's motivation and ability to trust other people including teachers, coaches and instructors. Simply put, this rewiring of the brain leads to a the "fight and flight" state (sympathetic nervous system being in control) becoming the baseline (or normal) instead of a response to contextual stressors (in "healthy" brains the parasympathetic nervous system also known as the "rest and digest state" is in control and is baseline).

The abnormal amount of cortisol released in a traumatised person effects various brain areas needed for learning, memory and emotional regulation including the hippocampus (involved in learning and memory and converting short-term memories to permanent memories), and frontal cortex region. This abnormal cortisol response also over activates the Amygdala (involved in fear, emotion, and memory), increases anxiety, triggers aphantasia (lack of cognitive visual ability which impacts memory storage and retrieval), triggers various emotional regulation difficulties, triggers Alexithymia (poor Interoception leading to poor understanding of one's own emotional experience), triggers insomnia and other sleep disturbances, worsens memory, overstimulates epinephrine and norepinephrine (leading to poorer motivation regulation), leads to poorer behaviours (such as "class clown" or aggressive behaviours) in classroom and other social settings and worsens learning capability overall.

There are many ideas that people in positions of teaching can implement to support the traumatised brain to learn effectively. Some of these include – group and individual learning programs, emotion regulation psychoeducation for teacher and students, journaling ideas and emotions, drawing ideas and emotions, channelling negative emotions into constructive goals, having an emotionally safe person and environment such as a teacher or mentor and having other supports in place or at least ideas in how to engage in those supports. Other supports include regular psychological assistance, social clubs such as sports, music, or tabletop gaming as well as regular sleep and eating habits.

Notes:

Learning Disorders – brief discussion

Learning disorders are a group of neurodevelopmental disorders that manifest during formal schooling, characterised by persistent and impairing difficulties in learning foundational academic skills for reading, writing, and/or mathematics. These are diagnosed when there are specific deficits in an individual's ability to perceive or process information efficiently and accurately. There must be significant impairment in the specified scholastic skill, and this impairment should not be due to sensory/motor deficits, poor teaching, lack of adequate stimulation, or any such external causes. This is a good definition, however, many external causes such as trauma can lead to a learning disorder developing as a trauma response. Learning disabilities can range in severity and may affect only one specific skill or a combination of skills. They are usually present from birth or early childhood and can persist throughout a person's life. Some people with learning disabilities may need accommodations to succeed academically and professionally, while others may be able to overcome their challenges with extra support and effort.

Research has suggested that approximately 10 percent of school aged children experience some form of learning difficulty, although this is often thought to be an under representation when compared to what teachers and instructors observe. The most common learning disorders diagnosed and observed in the western schooling system include – Intellectual Developmental Disorder (where a person experiences deficits in general mental abilities and impairment in everyday adaptive functioning compared to other people their own age), Language Disorder (difficulties in acquiring, using, comprehending and producing language compared to other people their own age), Speech Sound Disorder (difficulties in production of correct sounds), Auditory Processing Disorder (difficulties in understanding information provided verbally or through sounds), Stuttering difficulties, Social Communication Disorder (greater difficulties with the – social use of language, understanding and following social rules and adapting to social rule and language changes), Autism Spectrum Disorder, Attention Deficit Hyperactivity Disorder, Dyslexia (difficulties in reading, writing, and spelling), Dyscalculia (difficulties understanding number-based information and math) and Dysgraphia (difficulties with writing ability, including problems with letter formation/legibility, letter spacing, spelling, fine motor coordination, rate of writing, grammar, and composition).

As with most difficulties, if a person receives the right support, they can overcome and/or manage their difficulties and still achieve their goals. Many people considered successful in our western media have various learning difficulties and disorders but have still been able to achieve their goals. As well as the various supports available for children, there are also many supports for adults with learning difficulties available such as the 'Reading and Writing Hotline' in Australia. Personally, I have been able to use my differences in learning as a strength but have also had to create extra processes that other people often don't have to in order to be effective in my professional and personal tasks.

Notes:

Irlen Syndrome – brief discussion

Irlen Syndrome, also referred to as Meares-Irlen Syndrome, Scotopic Sensitivity Syndrome and Visual Stress, is a visual perception processing disorder, and is not an optical problem. It is a problem with the brain's ability to process visual information, often affecting specific colour wave lengths. This problem has a strong genetic component and is not able to be identified with optical assessments, standardised educational assessments or medical tests. In Australia a diagnosis of Irlen Syndrome can be suggested by professionals that have previous training in education, psychology, Occupational Therapy, speech therapy or other education or medical related fields and have registered with the AAIC (Australasian Association of Irlen Consultants).

Irlen Syndrome is considered controversial despite first being described in the early 1980s. This is because there is still not enough data and evidence to conclusively demonstrate the symptoms are separate to other mental and physical health conditions. Despite this, many people have benefited from seeking assistance. Symptoms of Irlen Syndrome include – sensitivity to light, reading difficulties, distortions to specific coloured print, spelling problems, delayed learning, concentration difficulties, behavioural problems, handwriting problems, depth perception difficulties, eye strain, headaches and migraines and greater levels of fatigue after schooling or academic work.

Irlen syndrome can be treated using tinted glasses or contact lenses, and coloured overlaps for books and screens for technology. This method works by filtering out specific light wavelengths to correct the defect in visual pathways. Individuals with Irlen syndrome will need to attend testing to determine the severity of the syndrome and if colour technology can eliminate the defect. The correct colour overlay for the individual will then be decided. Once the prescribed tinted glasses or contact lenses have arrived, individuals with Irlen syndrome often see a reduction in light sensitivity, headaches and fatigue and often report improvements in reading, depth perception, concentration, driving, and computer use ability.

Notes:

Conclusion

Human beings exhibit a remarkable diversity in learning styles, owing to their many individual differences. Identifying one's optimal learning approach not only facilitates the learning process but also fosters a sense of enjoyment and functional effectiveness. Moreover, this self-awareness equips individuals with tools to navigate obstacles with greater ease and resilience.

There are many different aspects to learning that can often be forgotten such as the best learning style combinations for each person, the sensory impacts on learning, the various internal and environmental factors regarding learning and understanding how best to learn in each context. Understanding how we learn, what our strengths are, and what extra assistance we benefit from ourselves, can help with understanding (logically and with empathy) another person's learning needs.

The are many ideas discussed in this book that can be expanded on by learning professionals or by the individual. As discussed throughout this book the many frameworks for learning and goal setting and the many ideas, need to be individualised where possible, to improve their efficacy for the individual. There are many resources in the Appendix section for people wanting to explore particular areas in more detail.

Appendix/References

Formal References

Abel, J. L., & Larkin, K. T. (1990). Anticipation of performance among musicians: Physiological arousal, confidence, and state-anxiety. Psychology of music, 18(2), 171-182.

Ackerman, D. (1991). A natural history of the senses. Vintage.

Aisbett, B. (2013). Fixing It: The Complete Survivor's Guide to Anxiety-Free Living. Harper Collins Inc.

Ambrose, S. A., Bridges, M. W., DiPietro, M., Lovett, M. C., & Norman, M. K. (2010). How learning works: Seven research-based principles for smart teaching. John Wiley & Sons.

American Psychiatric Association. (2013). Diagnostic and statistical manual of mental disorders (5th ed.).

Anderson, Lorin W., and David R. Krathwohl, eds. 2001. A Taxonomy for Learning, Teaching, and Assessing: A Revision of Bloom's Taxonomy of Educational Objectives. New York: Addison Wesley Longman, Inc.

Arden, J. B. (2010). Rewired Your Brain: Think Your Way to a Better Life. Wiley.

Armitage, C. J. (2009). Is there utility in the transtheoretical model?. British journal of health psychology, 14(2), 195-210.

Armstrong, P. (2010). Bloom's Taxonomy. Vanderbilt University Center for Teaching. Retrieved [January, 2024] from https://cft.vanderbilt.edu/guides-sub-pages/blooms-taxonomy/.

Armstrong, T. (2009). Multiple intelligences in the classroom. Ascd.

Ausubel, D. P. (2012). The acquisition and retention of knowledge: a cognitive view. Springer Science Business Media.

Azizan, M. T., Mellon, N., Ramli, R. M., & Yusup, S. (2018). Improving teamwork skills and enhancing deep learning via development of board game using cooperative learning method in Reaction Engineering course. Education for Chemical Engineers, 22, 1-13.

Bailie, J. M. (1984). Giant Book of Knowledge. Octopus Publishing Group.

Baker, M. (2007). Music moves brain to pay attention. Stanford Study Finds. Retrieved December, 15, 2015.

Bandura, A. (1977). Social learning theory. Englewood Cliffs, NJ: Prentice Hall.

Ben-David, S., Blitzer, J., Crammer, K., Kulesza, A., Pereira, F., & Vaughan, J. W. (2010). A theory of learning from different domains. Machine learning, 79, 151-175.

Bigger, B. B. (2012). Anita Marie Collins (Doctoral dissertation, The University of Melbourne).

Bokiev, D., Bokiev, U., Aralas, D., Ismail, L., & Othman, M. (2018). Utilizing music and songs to promote student engagement in ESL classrooms. International Journal of Academic Research in Business and Social Sciences, 8(12), 314–332

Bransford, J. D., & Johnson, M. K. (1972). Contextual prerequisites for understanding: Some investigations of comprehension and recall. Journal of verbal learning and verbal behavior, 11(6), 717-726.

Brewer, B.C. (2012). Music and learning: Integrating music in the classroom. Johns Hopkins School of Education.

Brod, G., Werkle-Bergner, M., & Shing, Y. L. (2013). The influence of prior knowledge on memory: a developmental cognitive neuroscience perspective. Frontiers in behavioral neuroscience, 7, 139.

Burgoyne, A. P., Sala, G., Gobet, F., Macnamara, B. N., Campitelli, G., & Hambrick, D. Z. (2016). The relationship between cognitive ability and chess skill: A comprehensive meta-analysis. Intelligence, 59, 72-83.

Burton, L., Westen, D., & Kowalski, R. (2006). Psychology: Australian and New Zealand Edition. John Wiley & Sons, Inc.

Burton, L., Westen, D., & Kowalski, R. (2008). Psychology 2: Australian and New Zealand Edition. John Wiley & Sons, Inc.

Bybee, R. W., Taylor, J. A., Gardner, A., Van Scotter, P., Powell, J. C., Westbrook, A., & Landes, N. (2006). The BSCS 5E instructional model: Origins and effectiveness. Colorado Springs, Co: BSCS, 5(88-98).

Carr, S. C., & Thompson, B. (1996). The effects of prior knowledge and schema activation strategies on the inferential reading comprehension of children with and without learning disabilities. Learning Disability Quarterly, 19(1), 48-61.

Case-Smith, J., Weaver, L. L., & Fristad, M. A. (2014). A systematic review of sensory processing interventions for children with autism spectrum disorders. *Autism: The International Journal of Research and Practice*.

Cattaneo, L., & Rizzolatti, G. (2009). The mirror neuron system. Archives of neurology, 66(5), 557-560.

Chaplan, J. P. (1970). Dictionary of Psychology. Dell Publishing.

Chen, W., & Zhao, J. (2022). Open the Black-box of "Informational Learning Style": Discussions Based-on Don Ihde's Phenomenology of Technology. Journal of East China Normal University (Educational Sciences), 40(10), 100.

Christ, S. (2013). 20 Surprising, Science-backed Health Benefits of Music. USA Today. Gannett, 17.

Cohen, M. J. (1993). Integrated ecology: The process of counseling with nature. The Humanistic Psychologist, 21(3), 277-295.

Collins, A. (2009). A boy's music ecosystem. Male voices: Stories of boys learning through making music.

Collins, A. (2014). Neuroscience, music education and the pre-service primary (elementary) generalist teacher. International Journal of Education & the Arts, 15(5).

Cowan, N. (2008). What are the differences between long-term, short-term, and working memory?. Progress in brain research, 169, 323-338.

Crawford, S., & Stucki, L. (1990). Peer review and the changing research record. Journal of the American Society for Information Science, 41(3), 223-228.

Dapretto, M., Davies, M.S., Pfiefer, J.H., Scott, A.A., Sigman, M., Bookheimer, S.Y., Iacoboni, M. (2006). Understanding Emotions in Others: Mirror Neuron Dysfunction in Children with Autism Spectrum Disorders. Nature Neuroscience, 9(1), 28–30.

Davey, B. (1983). Think aloud: Modeling the cognitive processes of reading comprehension. Journal of reading, 27(1), 44-47.

Demarin, V., & MOROVIĆ, S. (2014). Neuroplasticity. Periodicum biologorum, 116(2), 209-211.

Dewar, G. C. (2003). Innovation and social transmission in animals: A cost-benefit model of the predictive function of social and nonsocial cues. University of Michigan.

Doidge, N. (2008). The Brain that Changes Itself: Stories of Personal Triumph from the Frontiers of Brain Science.

Doran, G.T. (1981) There's a SMART Way to Write Management's Goals and Objectives. Journal of Management Review, 70, 35-36.

Drucker, P. F., (1954). "The Practice of Management". New York: Elsevier, : 109-110.

Duplechain, R., Reigner, R., & Packard, A. (2008). Striking differences: The impact of moderate and high trauma on reading achievement. Reading Psychology, 29(2), 117-136.

Eight Ways framework. (2009). NSW Department of Education initiative. https://www.8ways.online/

Foran, L. M. (2009). Listening to music: Helping children regulate their emotions and improve learning in the classroom. Educational Horizons, 88(1) 51-58.

Forehand, M. (2005). Bloom's taxonomy: Original and revised. Emerging perspectives on learning, teaching, and technology, 8, 41-44.

Frensch, P. A. (1998). One concept, multiple meanings: On how to define the concept of implicit learning. In M. A. Stadler & P. A. Frensch (Eds.), Handbook of implicit learning (pp. 47–104). Sage Publications, Inc.

Frieze, S. (2015). How Trauma Affects Student Learning and Behaviour. BU Journal of Graduate Studies in Education, 7(2), 27-34.

Gallese, V. (2006). Intentional attunement: A neurophysiological perspective on social cognition and its disruption in autism. Brain Research, 1079(1), 15-24

Gardner, H., & Hatch, T. (1989). Educational implications of the theory of multiple intelligences. Educational researcher, 18(8), 4-10.

Gardner, H. (1993). Multiple intelligences: The theory in practice. Basic books.

Geiger, G., Cattaneo, C., Galli, R., Pozzoli, U., Lorusso, M. L., Facoetti, A., & Molteni, M. (2008). Wide and diffuse perceptual modes characterize dyslexics in vision and audition. Perception, 37(11), 1745-1764.

Gerber, A. S., Green, D. P., Kaplan, E. H., Shapiro, I., Smith, R. M., & Massoud, T. (2014). The illusion of learning from observational research. Field experiments and their critics: Essays on the uses and abuses of experimentation in the social sciences, 9-32.

Goleman, D. (1996). Emotional Intelligence: Why it can matter more than IQ. Bloomsbury Publishing.

Gonzalez, M. F., & Aiello, J. R. (2019, January 28). More than meets the ear: Investigating how music affects cognitive task performance. Journal of Experimental Psychology: Applied. Advance online publication. http://dx.doi.org/10.1037/xap0000202

Gormally, C., Brickman, P., Hallar, B., & Armstrong, N. (2009). Effects of inquiry-based learning on students' science literacy skills and confidence. International journal for the scholarship of teaching and learning, 3(2), 16.

Greenberg, G. (2014). How new ideas in physics and biology influence developmental science. Research in Human Development, 11(1), 5-21.

Greene, R. (2013). Mastery. Penguin.

Greensfelder, L. (2009). Study Finds Brain Hub That Links Music, Memory and Emotion. UC Davis. Science & Technology. February, 23.

Hamasaki, H. (2020). Effects of diaphragmatic breathing on health: a narrative review. *Medicines*, *7*(10), 65.

Hambrick, D. Z., Campitelli, G., & Macnamara, B. N. (Eds.). (2017). The science of expertise: Behavioral, neural, and genetic approaches to complex skill. Routledge.

Hanfstingl, B., Arzenšek, A., Apschner, J., & Gölly, K. I. (2021). Assimilation and accommodation. European Psychologist.

Harmon-Jones, E., Harmon-Jones, C., & Levy, N. (2015). An action-based model of cognitive-dissonance processes. Current Directions in Psychological Science, 24(3), 184-189.

Harrison, S. D. (2007). Where have the boys gone? The perennial problem of gendered participation in music. British Journal of Music Education, 24(3), 267-280.

Hendrickx, S. (2010). The adolescent and adult neuro-diversity handbook: Asperger's syndrome, ADHD, dyslexia, dyspraxia, and related conditions. Jessica Kingsley Publishers.

Hmelo-Silver, C. E., Duncan, R. G., & Chinn, C. A. (2007). Scaffolding and achievement in problem-based and inquiry learning: a response to Kirschner, Sweller, and. Educational psychologist, 42(2), 99-107.

Jaycox, L. H., Langley, A. K., Stein, B., Wong, M., Sharma, P., Scott, M., & Schonlau, M. (2009). Support for students exposed to trauma: A pilot study. School Mental Health, 1(2), 49-60.

Jensen, P. S., Mrazek, D., Knapp, P. K., Steinberg, L., Pfeffer, C., Schowalter, J., & Shapiro, T. (1997). Evolution and revolution in child psychiatry: ADHD as a disorder of adaptation. Journal of the American Academy of Child & Adolescent Psychiatry, 36(12), 1672-1681.

Karpicke, J. D. (2012). Retrieval-based learning: Active retrieval promotes meaningful learning. Current Directions in Psychological Science, 21(3), 157-163.

Katzir, T., Hershko, S., & Halamish, V. (2013). The effect of font size on reading comprehension on second and fifth grade children: Bigger is not always better. PloS one, 8(9), e74061.

Key Learnings from Bigger Better Brains Educators Course 2020. 2024. Simply for Strings.

Kılavuz, Y. (2005). The effect of 5E learning method based on constructivist approach to the understanding of the concepts related to acids and bases of 10th graders. Post graduate Thesis, Institute of Science, Ankara.

Kimball, D. R., & Holyoak, K. J. (2000). Transfer and expertise. The Oxford handbook of memory, 109-122.

Kleingeld, A., van Mierlo, H., & Arends, L. (2011). "The Effect of Goal Setting on Group Performance: A Meta-analysis," Journal of Applied Psychology 96, no. 6: 1,289-1,304.

Kristenson, S. (2002). Alternatives to SMART goals. Found at www.developgoodhabits.com/

Kruk, R., Sumbler, K., & Willows, D. (2008). Visual processing characteristics of children with Meares–Irlen syndrome. Ophthalmic and Physiological Optics, 28(1), 35-46.

Lane, S. J., Mailloux, Z., Schoen, S., Bundy, A., May-Benson, T. A., Parham, L. D., ... & Schaaf, R. C. (2019). Neural foundations of ayres sensory integration®. Brain sciences, 9(7), 153.

Lawson, A. E., & Karplus, R. (2002). The learning cycle. In A love of discovery: Science education—The second career of Robert Karplus (pp. 51-76). Dordrecht: Springer Netherlands.

Lee, J. L., Nader, K., & Schiller, D. (2017). An update on memory reconsolidation updating. Trends in cognitive sciences, 21(7), 531-545.

Lertola, J., Park, A. (2002). Anatomy of Anxiety: What triggers it and how the body responds., Time Magazine.

Levitin, D. J. (2006). This is your brain on music: The science of a human obsession. Penguin.

Lohman, D. F., & Lakin, J. M. (2011). Intelligence and reasoning. The Cambridge handbook of intelligence, 419-441.

Louth, S., Wheeler, K., Jamieson-Proctor, R., & Sanderson, T. (2023). Stoking the Fires of Pre-service Educators through Aboriginal and Torres Strait Islander Ways of Learning. International Journal of Educational Innovation and Research, 2(2), 104-113.

McCann, T. (2011). *An evaluation of the effects of a training programme in Trauma Release Exercises on quality of life* (Master's thesis, University of Cape Town).

McGrath, P. (2004). The burden of RA RA positive: survivors' and hospice patients' reflection on maintaining a positive attitude to serious illness. Support Care Cancer, 12, 25-33.

McLaughlin, A. C., & Byrne, V. E. (2020). A fundamental cognitive taxonomy for cognition aids. Human Factors, 62(6), 865-873.

Mantle, S. (2001). The seven learning styles. Teaching/Learning Methods and Skills-Pedagogy.

Martin, G. N., Carlson, N. R., & Buskist, W. (2010). Psychology. *Fourth Edition*. Pearson Education.

Medina, J. (2009). Brain Rules: 12 Principles for Surviving and Thriving at Work, Home and School. Pear Press.

Miller, W. R., & Rollnick, S. (2012). Motivational interviewing: Helping people change. Guilford press.

Mills, M., Martino, W., & Lingard, B. (2007). Getting boys' education 'right': The Australian Government's Parliamentary Inquiry Report as an exemplary instance of recuperative masculinity politics. British journal of sociology of education, 28(1), 5-21.

Moran, D. J., & Ming, S. (2023). Finding your why and finding your way: An acceptance and commitment therapy workbook to help you identify what you care about and reach your goals. New Harbinger Publications.

Mottron, L. (2011). The power of autism. Nature, 479(7371), 33-35.

Murchie, G. (1999). The seven mysteries of life: an exploration in science & philosophy. Houghton Mifflin Harcourt.

Musacchia, G., Sams, M., Skoe, E., and Kraus, N. 2007. Musicians have enhanced subcortical auditory and audiovisual processing of speech and music. Proc. Natl. Acad. Sci. U.S.A. 104:15894–8. doi: 10.1073/pnas.0701498104

Nishikawa, T., & Motter, A. E. (2016). Symmetric states requiring system asymmetry. Physical review letters, 117(11), 114101.

Noonan, W. C., & Moyers, T. B. (1997). Motivational interviewing. Journal of Substance Misuse, 2(1), 8-16.

Oberman, L. M., & Ramachandran, V. S. (2007). The simulating social mind: The role of the mirror neuron system and simulation in the social and communicative deficits of autism spectrum disorders. Psychological Bulletin, 133(2), 310-327.

Oleg, Y. (2015). Interdisciplinary Aspects of Learning: Physics and Psychology. Universal Journal of Educational Research, 3(11), 810-814.

On, F. R., Jailani, R., Norhazman, H., & Zaini, N. M. (2013, March). Binaural beat effect on brainwaves based on EEG. In 2013 IEEE 9th International Colloquium on Signal Processing and its Applications (pp. 339-343). IEEE.

Pan, S. C., & Rickard, T. C. (2018). Transfer of test-enhanced learning: Meta-analytic review and synthesis. Psychological bulletin, 144(7), 710.

Pattie, S. T. (2023). My Eclectic Human Body: Eclectic Knowledge Journey (Summaries, Principles & Exercises). Ingram Content Group Australia Pty Ltd.

Peale, N. V. (1990). The Power of Positive Thinking. Ebury Press.

Peeck, J., Van den Bosch, A. B., & Kreupeling, W. J. (1982). Effect of mobilizing prior knowledge on learning from text. Journal of Educational Psychology, 74(5), 771.

Plomin, R., & Rowe, D. C. (1977). A twin study of temperament in young children. The Journal of Psychology, 97(1), 107-113.

Popper, K. (2005). The logic of scientific discovery. Routledge.

PosNER, G. J., Strike, K. A., Hewson, P. W., & Gertzog, W. A. (1982). Toward a theory of conceptual change. Science education, 66(2), 211-227.

Preston, A. R., & Eichenbaum, H. (2013). Interplay of hippocampus and prefrontal cortex in memory. Current biology, 23(17), R764-R773.

Purves, D., Augustine, G. J., et. al. (2004). Neuroscience: Third Edition., Sinauer Associates.

Rauscher, F. H., Shaw, G. L., and Ky, K. N. 1995. Listening to Mozart enhances spatial-temporal reasoning: towards a neurophysiological basis. Neurosci. Lett. 185:44–7

Roediger, H. L., & Butler, A. C. (2011). The critical role of retrieval practice in long-term retention. Trends in cognitive sciences, 15(1), 20-27.

Rowland, C. A. (2014). The effect of testing versus restudy on retention: a meta-analytic review of the testing effect. Psychological bulletin, 140(6), 1432.

Ruiz-Martín, H., & Bybee, R. W. (2022). The cognitive principles of learning underlying the 5E Model of Instruction. International journal of STEM Education, 9(1), 21.

Saarikallio, S., and Erkkila, J. (2007). The role of music in adolescents' mood regulation. Psychology of Music. 35 (1), 88-109.

Saddawi-Konefka, D., Baker, K., Guarino, A., Burns, S. M., Oettingen, G., Gollwitzer, P. M., & Charnin, J. E. (2017). Changing resident physician studying behaviors: A randomized, comparative effectiveness trial of goal setting versus use of WOOP. Journal of graduate medical education, 9(4), 451-457.

Sadock, B. J., Sadock, V. A., & Ruiz, P. (2015). Kaplan & Sadock's Synopsis of Psychiatry: Behavioural Sciences/Clinical Psychiatry. *Eleventh Edition*.

Scaer, R. (2011). The Body Bears the Burden: Trauma, Dissociation, and Disease.

Schlaug, G. 2009. "Music, musicians, and brain plasticity," in Oxford Handbook of Music Psychology, eds S. Hallam, I. Cross and M. Thaut (Oxford: Oxford University Press), 197–207.

Schunk, D. (2016). Learning theories: An educational perspective. Pearson.

Shafique, M. (2015). Are we doomed not to reach our goals despite how optimistic we are?. Read on LinkedIn.

Shafique, M. (2015). Pursuit vs End Result – What's more Important?. Read on LinkedIn.

Shafique, M. (2015). The Fear of Failing and How to Reclaim It. Read on LinkedIn.

Shafique, M. (2015). The origin of Goal-Setting. Read on LinkedIn.

Shapiro, F., Wesselmann, D., & Mevissen, L. (2017). Eye movement desensitization and reprocessing therapy (EMDR). Evidence-based treatments for trauma related disorders in children and adolescents, 273-297.

Sitler, H. C. (2009). Teaching with awareness: The hidden effects of trauma on learning. Clearing House: A Journal of Education Strategies, Issues, and Ideas, 82(3), 119-124.

Snyder, A. N. Mirror Neurons and Their Effects on Social-Emotional Learning. Medford Public Schools.

Snyder, D. M. (1990). On the relation between psychology and physics. The Journal of Mind and Behavior, 1-17.

Sperling, A. P. (1992). Psychology Made Simple. Butterworth-Heinemann Limited.

Stampi, C. (1989). Polyphasic sleep strategies improve prolonged sustained performance: a field study on 99 sailors. Work & Stress, 3(1), 41-55.

Stampi, C. (1992). Evolution, chronobiology, and functions of polyphasic and ultrashort sleep: main issues. Why we nap: evolution, chronobiology, and functions of polyphasic and ultrashort sleep, 1-20.

Stillman, J., Anderson, L., Arellano, A., Wong, P. L., Berta-Avila, M., Alfaro, C., & Struthers, K. (2013). Putting PACT in context and context in PACT: Teacher educators collaborating around program-specific and shared learning goals. Teacher Education Quarterly, 40(4), 135-157.

Sull, D & Escobari. (2005). "Success Against the Odds: What Brazilian Champions Teach Us About Thriving in Unpredictable Markets" (Rio de Janeiro and Cambridge, Massachusetts: Editora Campus.

Sull, D., Kang H., Thompson, N., and Hu, L. (2018). "Trade-offs in Firm Culture? Nope, You Can Have It All," MIT Sloan School of Management working paper.

Sull, D., & Sull, C. (2018). With Goals, FAST Beats SMART. *The Strategic Agility Project / Research Highlights*.

Temmerman, N. (2006). Improving school music education: We all have a part to play. Professional Educator, 5(1), 34-39.

Uttal, W. R. (2014). Time, Space, and Number in Physics and Psychology (Psychology Revivals). Psychology Press.

Van der Kolk. B. A. (2015). The Body Keeps the Score: Mind, Brain and Body in the Transformation of Trauma. Penguin Books.

Verweij, K. J., Mosing, M. A., Zietsch, B. P., & Medland, S. E. (2012). Estimating heritability from twin studies. Statistical human genetics: methods and protocols, 151-170.

Vidyadharan, V., & Tharayil, H. M. (2019). Learning disorder or learning disability: Time to rethink. Indian Journal of Psychological Medicine, 41(3), 276-278.

Vivanti, G., & Rogers, S. J. (2014). Autism and the mirror neuron system: Insights from learning and teaching. Philosophical Transactions of the Royal Society B: Biological Sciences, 369(1644), 20130184.

Warren, E. M. (1998). Impact of an initial learning disabilities diagnosis in college on an adult's sense of self as a lifelong learner. University of Georgia.

Washburne, J. N. (1936). The definition of learning. *Journal of Educational Psychology, 27*(8), 603–611. https://doi.org/10.1037/h0060154

Wenzel, K., & Reinhard, M. A. (2021). Does the end justify the means? Learning tests lead to more negative evaluations and to more stress experiences. Learning and Motivation, 73, 101706.

Wheeler, D. (2005). A taxonomy for learning, teaching and assessing.

White, H. A., & Shah, P. (2011). Creative style and achievement in adults with attention-deficit/hyperactivity disorder. Personality and individual differences, 50(5), 673-677.

Williams, J., Whiten, A., Suddendorf, T., & Perrett, D. (2001). Imitation, mirror neurons and autism. Neuroscience & Biobehavioral Reviews, 25(4), 287-295.

Woloshyn, V. E., Paivio, A., & Pressley, M. (1994). Use of elaborative interrogation to help students acquire information consistent with prior knowledge and information inconsistent with prior knowledge. Journal of Educational Psychology, 86(1), 79.

Young, S. H. (2019). Ultralearning. NINE, 2, 1.

Course/Degree/CPD References

Author of 'My Eclectic Human Body'

Bachelor of Psychology group Honours – James Cook University

Certificate 3, 4, Master Trainer – Australian Institute of Fitness

Diploma Counselling – TAFE North

Psychology CPD's used in this book:

- Arielle Schwartz – PESI Australia – Complex Trauma Treatment
- Bessel van der Kolk – PESI – Online Certificate regarding 'Rewiring the Brain: Neurofeedback
- Black Dog Institute – REACH Facilitator Training
- Blue Knot Foundation – A Three-Phased Approach – 'Working Therapeutically with Complex Trauma Clients'
- Community Training Australia – Workshop for 'Body Therapies'
- Community Training Australia – Workshop for 'Understanding Grief and Loss'
- Comorbidity Guidelines online training – Management of Co-occurring alcohol and other drug and mental health conditions in alcohol and other drug treatment settings
- GriffinOT – Sensory Processing Aware Level 1
- GriffinOT – Sensory Processing Aware Level 2
- GriffinOT – Sensory Processing Aware Level 3
- Headspace online training – Developmental Disorders in Young People

- Insight Alcohol and other drug training and workforce development Queensland – Modules 1-6
- Jennifer Sweeton – PESI Australia – PTSD Trauma treatment – EMDR, CBT and Somatic-Based Interventions
- Jon Kabat-Zinn – PESI – Online Certificate regarding 'Mindfulness, Healing and Transformation: The Pain and the Promise of Befriending the Full Catastrophe
- Leslie Korn – PESI – Online Certificate regarding 'Nutrition for Mental Health'
- Linda Curran – PESI – Online Certificate regarding 'Master Clinician Series The Adverse Childhood Experiences Study
- Mental Health First Aid Australia – Standard Mental Health First Aid Facilitator fourth edition course
- Mental Health First Aid Australia – Webcast 'MHFA Auditory Hallucination Simulation'
- Online training NCETA – Ice: Training for Frontline Workers Certificate of Completion modules 1-7
- PESI Australia – Autism and Sensory Processing Disorder
- PESI Australia – Autism Meltdowns in Children and Adolescents
- PESI Australia – High-Functioning Autism
- Stephen Porges PhD – PESI Australia – Clinical Applications of the Polyvagal Theory

Advanced Master Herbalist Diploma Online – Centre of Excellence

Yoga for Mental Health – Rewire Therapy – Student

Tai Chi for Arthritis Course

White Tiger Qi Gong Courses

- Trinity System Chinese Medicine Fundamentals
- Fascia Foundations Course
- 5 Element QiYo Course
- Qi Gong for Worry and Anxiety

Informal References

AMN Academy Holistic Health Coach Course

PNI Global Awareness – PNI course and Wellness Management information

Various Podcasts and articles by Dr. Rhonda Patrick - www.foundmyfitness.com

Aucademy6195. (n.d.). Aucademy. YouTube. Retrieved 2022-2023, from https://www.youtube.com/@aucademy6195

DifferingMinds. (n.d.). Differing Minds. YouTube. Retrieved from 2023, from https://www.youtube.com/@DifferingMinds

FoundMyFitness. (n.d.). FoundMyFitness. YouTube. Retrieved from 2020-2023, from https://www.youtube.com/@FoundMyFitness

HowtoADHD. (n.d.). How to ADHD. YouTube. Retrieved from 2022-2023, from https://www.youtube.com/@HowtoADHD

Kurzgesagt. (n.d.) Kurzgesagt – In a Nutshell. YouTube. Retrieved from 2015-2023, from https://www.youtube.com/@kurzgesagt

Neuroscientificallychallenged. (n.d.). Neuroscientifically Challenged. YouTube. Retrieved from 2021-2022, from https://www.youtube.com/@Neuroscientificallychallenged

Nicabm. (n.d.). NICABM. YouTube. Retrieved from 2020-2023, from https://www.youtube.com/@nicabm

SciShow. (n.d.). SciShow. YouTube. Retrieved from 2015-2023, from https://www.youtube.com/@SciShow

Socialworkact8660. (n.d.). Social Work & ACT. YouTube. Retrieved from 2020-2022, from https://www.youtube.com/@socialworkact8660

TEDEd. (n.d.). TED-Ed. YouTube. Retrieved from 2015-2023, from https://www.youtube.com/@TEDEd

Treforall312. (n.d.) TRE FOR ALL. YouTube. Retrieved from 2021-2023, from https://www.youtube.com/@treforall312

Warrenerica1. (n.d.) Erica Warren. YouTube. Retried 2023, from https://www.youtube.com/@warrenerica1

Previous Influential Professionals

Gym Manager – Donna Hartley

Long Term Personal Training Client – Janelle Fox

Mental Health Facilitator – Philippa Harris

Mental Health Manager – Alison Fairleigh

Mental Health Manager – Cassandra Parry

Personal Training Course Instructor – Rebecca Leddy

Personal Training Manager / Zen Do Kai Karate / BJC Muay Thai Instructor – Marco Vogel

Pilates Mentor – Kat Syzmanski

Psychology Manager – Alana Bowen

Psychology Supervisor – Gayle Roe

Psychology Supervisor – Kirsten Seymour

Science Teacher / Itosu Shito Ryu Karate Instructor – Murray Burrows

Wing Chun Instructor – Pablo Cardenas

Various other people and professionals who assisted in my learning journey.

www.ingramcontent.com/pod-product-compliance
Lightning Source LLC
Chambersburg PA
CBHW072123020426
42334CB00018B/1689